Mother Goose's Golden Christmas

A Family Musical

Book, music and lyrics by

DAVID WOOD

With sincere thanks to
John Hole
for whom this is my tenth
commissioned play, and without
whose confidence, help and
encouragement I might have
given up after the first

SAMUEL FRENCH

LONDON
NEW YORK SYDNEY TORONTO HOLLYWOOD

MOTHER GOOSE'S GOLDEN CHRISTMAS

First presented at the Queen's Theatre, Hornchurch, on the 19th December 1977, with the following cast of characters:

Mother Goose	Brian Hewlett
Little Jack Horner	David Brenchley
Little Bo Peep	Deirdre Dee
Little Miss Muffet	Nicolette Marvin
Little Tommy Tucker	Lennox Greaves
Little Polly Flinders	Patience Tomlinson
Big Bad Wolf	Jack Chissick
Bigger Badder Wolf	Mike Maynard
Fairy Lethargia	Penny Jones
The Goose	Isobil Nisbet
The Giant	Tim Pearce
The Spider	
The Monster Of The Moat	Caroline Swift
Humpty Dumpty	

The play directed by Paul Tomlinson

Settings by David Knapman

Act I Scene 1 The Book—home of the Nursery Rhyme characters
  Scene 2 The Forest/Spider's Lair
  Scene 3 The Book
  Scene 4 The Forest, without the Spider's Lair
Act II Scene 1 The Forest (optional scene)
  Scene 2 Entrance to the Giant's Castle
  Scene 3 In the Moat—under water
  Scene 4 Entrance to the Giant's Castle
  Scene 5 The Giant's Workshop
  Scene 6 In the Sky
  Scene 7 The Book

As the play is based upon the well-known collection of Nursery Rhymes called "Mother Goose's Nursery Rhymes", the ideal period in which to set it is Victorian, with all the settings and costumes resembling a beautiful Victorian children's book.

CHARACTERS

Mother Goose
The purveyor of nursery rhymes, probably the "dame" part, lovable old lady, looking after her nursery rhyme "family".

Little Bo Peep
Weepy girl (because she is always losing her sheep!). Dressed in red (for reason which will become apparent).

Little Tommy Tucker
Fat, usually hungry, boy—sings for his supper.

Little Miss Muffet
The most imaginative of the "family"—her stories of meeting fearsome spiders are taken with a pinch of salt by the others.

Little Jack Horner
The nearest we get to a "Simple Simon" or "Idle Jack" part. Limited intelligence because his sole purpose in life is sitting in corners putting his thumb in and pulling plums out.

Little Polly Flinders
Grubby, skinny girl dressed in rags—the skivvy who cooks and cleans; but not looked down on or even discontented with her lot—this is her role in life and she enjoys it. Very shy—whispers a lot.

The Goose
Lovable, mute bird, must be capable of pathos, but humour as well; mimes to convey her thoughts, often interpreted by the audience.

The Big Bad Wolf
A small, rather nervous villain.

The Bigger Badder Wolf
A larger, rather confident villain.

Giant Bossyboots (could be played by the same actor)
The Wolves' employer. Ruthless, unsuccessful alchemist whose only aim is to make gold.

The Spider
Frightening frightener.

Fairy Lethargia
A lumpy, sleepy, reluctant fairy, who only emerges at Christmas time to sit on the Christmas tree. She *can* do magic spells, but only under pressure.

The Monster Of The Moat
A non-speaking monster, the guardian of the Giant's Castle. Probably similar to the Loch Ness Monster and in segments, which divide. The Monster could be played by Giant, Big Bad Wolf, Bigger Badder Wolf, The Goose, and/or others.

Humpty Dumpty
A last minute appearance—preferably played by a child.

MUSICAL NUMBERS

ACT I

1.	**We Wish You A Merry Christmas**	Little Miss Muffet, Little Jack Horner, Little Bo Peep, Little Tommy Tucker, Little Polly Flinders.
2.	**Once Upon A Time**	Mother Goose, Little Miss Muffet, Little Jack Horner, Little Bo Peep, Little Tommy Tucker, Little Polly Flinders.
3.	**The Song Of The Goose**	Little Tommy Tucker, Mother Goose, Little Miss Muffet, Little Jack Horner, Little Bo Peep, Little Polly Flinders (and the Goose).
4.	**With A Huff And A Puff**	Big Bad Wolf, Bigger Badder Wolf.
5.	**My Big Moment**	Little Miss Muffet.
6.	**Getting Ready For Christmas**	Mother Goose, Little Jack Horner, Little Bo Peep, Little Tommy Tucker, Little Polly Flinders.
7.	**Sheep, Sheep**	Little Bo Peep, Little Jack Horner, Little Tommy Tucker, Little Polly Flinders.
7A.	**My Big Moment** (reprise)	Little Bo Peep.
8.	**Fairy Lethargia's Magic Spell**	Fairy Lethargia.
9.	**Off To The Rescue**	Mother Goose, Little Miss Muffet, Little Jack Horner, Little Bo Peep, Little Tommy Tucker, Little Polly Flinders, Fairy Lethargia.

Act II

9A.	**Off To The Rescue** (reprise)	Mother Goose, Little Miss Muffet, Little Jack Horner, Little Bo Peep, Little Tommy Tucker, Little Polly Flinders.
9B.	**Fairy Lethargia's Magic Spell** (reprise)	Fairy Lethargia.
9C.	**My Big Moment** (reprise)	Little Polly Flinders.
10.	**Music: Underwater Sequence** (including **My Big Moment**)	
10A.	**Fairy Lethargia's Magic Spell** (reprise)	Fairy Lethargia.
11.	**When You're Feeling Worried**	Mother Goose, Little Miss Muffet, Little Tommy Tucker, Little Bo Peep, Little Polly Flinders, Fairy Lethargia.
12.	**Fee Fi Fo Fum**	Giant, Big Bad Wolf, Bigger Badder Wolf.
12A.	**My Big Moment** (reprise)	Little Jack Horner.
12B.	**Fairy Lethargia's Magic Spell** (reprise)	Fairy Lethargia.
13.	**Music: Flying Home Sequence** and **Her Big Moment**	Mother Goose, Little Jack Horner, Fairy Lethargia.
13A.	**Getting Ready For Christmas** (reprise)	Little Miss Muffet, Little Bo Peep, Little Tommy Tucker, Little Polly Flinders, joined by Mother Goose and Little Jack Horner.
14.	**Happy Christmas, Mother Goose**	Little Miss Muffet, Little Jack Horner, Little Bo Peep, Little Tommy Tucker, Little Polly Flinders, Fairy Lethargia (and the Goose).
15.	**Humpty Dumpty Sat On A Wall**	Humpty Dumpty.
16.	**Mother Goose's Golden Christmas**	The Company.

ACT I

SCENE 1

The Book. Home of the Nursery Rhyme characters. Dawn, Christmas Eve

This is their equivalent of a house; indeed it has a door, and maybe windows. It is suggested that the Book is three-quarters open, the covers facing the audience. On the front cover is the title—"Mother Goose's Golden Christmas Annual", with perhaps a picture representing Mother Goose flying on a Goose, accompanied by several young people. As perhaps the ideal time in which to set the play is Victorian, the design of the cover could well be in the style of one of the famous children's book illustrations of the period—e.g. Arthur Rackham or Kate Greenaway. It may be considered a good idea to start with the tabs already out, so that the audience can see the Book and its title before the House Lights go down. Alternatively, a painting of the Book on a gauze front cloth would give the magical possibility of "mixing through" to the real Book

Music, as the Lights come up on the Book

The door of the book opens and, surreptitiously, Little Miss Muffet creeps out, yawns and stretches, and looks both ways to see if anyone is coming. She beckons, and Little Jack Horner tiptoes out. They greet each other with excitement but no noise. Then Little Polly Flinders emerges, sweeping with a broom. The others shush her with a finger to their mouths and take away the broom, leaning it against the book. As the three huddle together, as though discussing a secret plan, Little Tommy Tucker comes out, eating a large sausage or a piece of pie, and not looking where he is going. He bumps into the group, who turn on him and shush him. Finally, Little Bo Peep, with her shepherdess's crook, comes out, ignoring the others but looking into the early morning light—in the hope of seeing her lost sheep. She shrugs her disappointment as Little Jack Horner takes away her crook and leads her to the others. This section should not take long. The idea is not to set up the individual characters, but rather to convey the fact that these five people live in the book, and, early this morning, having just woken up, are up to something secret

Little Miss Muffet shuts the door, and in fairly soft voices they sing.

SONG 1: **We Wish You A Merry Christmas**

During the song the children bring forward a Christmas tree and, setting it to one side of the stage, start to decorate it with tinsel and baubles, etc., which they take from a largish box labelled "Decorations", and which they wheel on for the purpose. Occasionally someone checks that no one is coming out of the door—the idea being, as we shall soon discover, that the children are doing this as a surprise for Mother Goose

Little Miss Muffet
Little Jack Horner
Little Bo Peep   *(singing)*
Little Tommy Tucker
Little Polly Flinders

> We wish you a Merry Christmas
> We wish you a Merry Christmas
> We wish you a Merry Christmas
> And a Happy New Year.
>
> Good tidings we bring
> To you and your kin
> We wish you a Merry Christmas
> And a Happy New Year.
>
> Now bring us some figgy pudding
> Now bring us some figgy pudding
> Now bring us some figgy pudding
> And bring some out here.
>
> We wish you a Merry Christmas
> We wish you a Merry Christmas

At this point the Christmas tree lights go on and the Children react happily

> We wish you a Merry Christmas

Little Tommy Tucker is pushed forward. He gives a good tug on the bell-rope. The bell rings

> And a Happy New Year.

Giggling with excitement, the Children hide to wait for the reaction

After a short pause, we hear Mother Goose's voice as she comes to answer the door, hurriedly putting on a dressing-gown

Mother Goose Who on earth can that be at this unearthly hour? (*She opens the door and steps out, and sees the lit-up tree. She gasps.*) Ah ...! Look what's grown in the night. An electric light tree. Someone must have planted a bulb!

The Children pop out from hiding, making Mother Goose jump. They gather round

Children Tara! Surprise, surprise! Happy Christmas, Mother Goose, etc.
Mother Goose Oh, little ones. All I can say is ... (*Suddenly*) Aaaaaah!

All jump

Little Tommy Tucker What's the matter, Mother Goose?
Mother Goose You're standing on my foot, Tommy dear.
Little Tommy Tucker Oh. Sorry. (*He moves*)
Mother Goose Thank you, dear, and thank you, all of you, for such a lovely seasonal surprise. But haven't you forgotten something?

Little Miss Muffet What?

Mother Goose I'm not sure. But somehow it doesn't look complete ..

The Children all think hard. Mother Goose suddenly sees the audience

Oh ...! (*To the audience*) Good morning. Hallo. Look, little ones, visitors. You're jolly early. I'm not even dressed yet. I don't usually open the door in my dressing-gown.

Little Jack Horner I didn't know you *had* a door in your dressing-gown. Tara!

Mother Goose Thank you, Jack. Anyway—(*to the audience*)—now you're here, I'm Mother Goose and I look after all the nursery rhyme children and we all live in this big Book, and I know there's something missing off that Christmas tree. Can *you* spot it?

The audience is encouraged to shout out that there is no fairy on the Christmas tree

Of course. That's it. They're right! The fairy. Where is she?

Little Bo Peep She only works at Christmas. Sleeps the rest of the year.

Mother Goose What a lazy fairy! Hibernating like a hedgehog. Anyone remember her name?

Little Polly Flinders raises her hand

Well, Polly?

Little Polly Flinders whispers in Mother Goose's ear, then smiles shyly

That's right. Fairy Lethargia. We'd better give her an alarm call and wake her up. After three. One, two, three.

All (*calling*) Fairy Lethargia.

No reaction

Mother Goose One, two, three.

All (*calling*) Fairy Lethargia.

No reaction

Mother Goose We need a few more decibels, I reckon. (*To the audience*) How about all joining in? Would you do that? Thank you. One, two, three.

All (*including the audience*) Fairy Lethargia.

Mother Goose And again. One, two, three.

All Fairy Lethargia.

Suddenly, a large yawn, accompanied perhaps by a drum roll, heralds the awakening of Fairy Lethargia. She crawls, unfairylike and anything but dainty, out of the decorations box. She holds a wand, complete with star on the end. She cannot stop yawning. This could possibly be accompanied by pretty, tinkling fairy music to point up the irony

Fairy Lethargia Oh no, it's not Christmas time again already, is it? (*She gives a huge yawn*)

Mother Goose Yes. And you're late, Lethargia.

Fairy Lethargia I'm sorry, I—ooh. (*Suddenly she sees the audience and makes* *an attempt to do a fairy balletic-type movement as she goes into rhyming couplets)*

Hallo, hallo, 'tis Christmas Eve and I am Fairy Lethargia,
My wand and spells and magic powers are here to watch and guardjya
Throughout the festive season my eyes on you I'll keep (*Yawning*)
Except when they start shutting, 'cos I need my beauty sleep. (*She falls asleep on her feet*)

Mother Goose One, two, three.
All (*calling*) Fairy Lethargia.

Fairy Lethargia jumps awake

Fairy Lethargia Oh no, it's not Christmas time again already, is it? (*She gives a huge yawn*)
Mother Goose Yes, it is.
Little Miss Muffet And you're meant to be on the tree.
Fairy Lethargia I'm not sitting on that tree. It's all prickly. And I might drop off.
Little Jack Horner That's your trouble—you're *always* dropping off. Tara!
Fairy Lethargia Cheek. Tell you what; we'll compromise. (*She waves her wand*)

My magic wand looks like a star, I'll stick it on the tree
And like a beacon burning bright, it'll make you think of me.

(*She arranges her wand on the tree*)

Return I shall for turkey, for Christmas pud and booze
Till then I think I'll say ta ta and have a little snooze.

She nips back into the decorations box, yawns and vanishes from sight. N.B. It may well be advisable for the box to extend a little into the wings, so that Fairy Lethargia can escape through one side to the wings between appearances

Mother Goose Charming. Daintiness personified. She works too hard, that's her trouble. A twelve-hour year. She's the same every Christmas. Do you remember, little ones, when ... (*She breaks off, then turns to the audience*) Oh, I'm sorry. How rude. I haven't even introduced my family to you, have I? Tell you what, let's see if you can guess who they all are—because ...

SONG 2: **Once Upon A Time**

Little Bo Peep	It
	Really won't surprise us
Little Jack Horner	If you recognize us
All the children	From a nursery rhyme
Mother Goose	And I'm sure you've heard them
	Or even learnt them
	Once upon a time.

The Children act out each other's story as appropriate. First, Little Bo Peep comes forward

Mother Goose	Here's a girl all pale and wan
	And she's crying, so something's wrong
Little Bo Peep	I can't help but weep
	I've lost all my sheep
	And don't know where they've gone.

The music continues

Mother Goose (*speaking to the audience*) Who is she?

The audience may give her an answer. She adlibs her thanks

All	She's
	Little Bo Peep
	Little Bo Peep
	From the nursery rhyme
	Little Bo Peep
	You must have learnt it
	Once upon a time.

Little Jack Horner	I was eating Christmas pie
	In the corner, then—who knows why?—
Mother Goose	He put in his thumb
	And pulled out a plum—
Little Jack Horner	What a good boy am I!

Again Mother Goose asks the audience who he is

All	He's
	Little Jack Horner
	Little Jack Horner
	From the nursery rhyme
	Little Jack Horner
	You must have learnt it
	Once upon a time.

Mother Goose	Here's a girl you'll know, I s'pose
	In the cinders she warmed her toes
All (*except Mother Goose and Little Polly Flinders*)	Her mother then caught her
	And told off her daughter
	For spoiling her new clothes.

The audience shout out who it is

All	She's
	Little Polly Flinders
	Little Polly Flinders
	From the nursery rhyme
	Little Polly Flinders
	You must have learnt it
	Once upon a time.

Little Tommy Tucker	Now bring me some figgy pudding

	Please bring me some figgy pudding—
	I am singing for my supper
Mother Goose	What shall we give him?
All (*except Little*	
Tommy Tucker)	White bread and butter
Little Tommy Tucker	It's no wonder
	I get fat
Mother Goose	Who can tell me ...
	Who is that?

The audience shout out the answer

All	He's
	Little Tommy Tucker
	Little Tommy Tucker
	From the nursery rhyme
	Little Tommy Tucker
	I'm sure you learnt it
	Once upon a time.

Little Miss Muffet	In the forest yesterday
	I was eating my curds and whey
Mother Goose	Along came a spider
	Who sat down beside her
Little Miss Muffet	And frightened me away.

The audience call out her name

All	She's
	Little Miss Muffet
	Little Miss Muffet
	From the nursery rhyme
	Little Miss Muffet
	I'm sure you learnt it
	Once upon a ...

	Little Miss Muffet
	Little Tommy Tucker
	Little Polly Flinders
	Little Jack Horner
	Little Bo Peep
	I'm sure you learnt them
Girls	Once upon a time
Boys	Once upon a time
Girls	Once upon a time
Boys	Once upon a time
All	Once upon a time

Mother Goose There you are, I told you you knew them all already! Right, little ones, breakfast time. (*She calls loudly*) Polly!

Little Polly Flinders comes forward shyly

Little Polly Flinders (*whispering*) Yes, Mother Goose?
Mother Goose Put the kettle on.

Music, as the Children revolve the Book, to reveal a room the other side. It is a kitchen with a large dining-table and a hearth complete with cinders, hob and traditional-style kettle. The Christmas tree and decorations box remains at the side of the stage. N.B. The revolve of the Book could take place during the last chorus of the song. Little Polly Flinders puts the kettle on. Mother Goose and the others sit at the table. Mother Goose pours herself some cereal from a packet or jar, and passes it down the line. First Little Jack Horner, then Little Miss Muffet pour themselves some; then Little Tommy Tucker pours all the remaining cereal on to his plate. The music stops as Little Bo Peep—on the end—bursts into tears. N.B. This section should be played at a fair speed

Little Jack Horner Oh, stop being weedy, Bo Peep.
Little Bo Peep I'm not being weedy. Tommy's taken all the cereal, the selfish pig.
Little Tommy Tucker I'm a growing boy.
Little Bo Peep Growing? Huh. If you grow any more you'll burst. Like a fat balloon.
Mother Goose Stop arguing, you two. Bo Peep, there's more cereal in the cupboard. So stop crying. Tommy, go and fetch her some.

Little Tommy Tucker does so

Little Miss Muffet She's always crying.
Little Bo Peep So would you if you kept losing your sheep. (*She starts sobbing again*)
Little Miss Muffet That's nothing compared with having to fight off great monster spiders every day.
Little Jack Horner So you say.
Little Miss Muffet What's that meant to mean?
Little Jack Horner Well, *we* never see these giant spiders of yours. *No one* sees them except you.
Little Miss Muffet Are you suggesting I invent them?
Little Jack Horner No. I'm just saying I've never seen one.
Little Bo Peep That's because he sits at home all day putting in his thumb and pulling out plums. What a waste of time.
Little Tommy Tucker No, it's not. They're very nice plums.
Little Bo Peep Well, we all know you're a greedy hog who never stops stuffing his face.
Little Tommy Tucker I'd rather be a greedy hog who never stops stuffing his face than one of your miserable stupid sheep who keep wandering off ...

Little Bo Peep is about to retaliate. Mother Goose interrupts

Mother Goose Ting-a-ling-a-ling-a-ling. End of Round One. That's enough. It's Christmas, time of good cheer. Now, what's the matter, little ones?

All the Children start to react angrily to the phrase "little ones". Then they think better of it. Silence

Eh?

Little Polly Flinders brings everyone a mug of tea

Thank you, Little Polly.

All the Children look at one another as if to say—"there you are". Little Polly Flinders sits

What have I said now?

Little Polly Flinders (*whispering*) Little.
Mother Goose Little?
Little Jack Horner Sorry, Mother Goose, but we're all getting a bit fed up with being "Little". *Little* Jack Horner.
Little Miss Muffet *Little* Miss Muffet.
Little Bo Peep We're all "Little".
Little Tommy Tucker And we always have to do the same old "little" things.
Little Jack Horner Day after day after day.
Little Polly Flinders (*whispering*) That's why we argue sometimes. It gives us something else to think about.

The others nod

Mother Goose I see. But, children, your nursery rhymes are so popular. Everyone knows them. You can't just stop doing what you do in them and start doing something else. People expect nursery rhymes to carry on for ever.
Little Jack Horner But I'm fed up with sitting in corners pulling out plums. There must be something more to life than that.
Little Bo Peep And I don't *enjoy* losing my sheep all the time. (*She starts to cry*)
Little Polly Flinders (*whispering*) I'd like to get away from my dirty old cinders sometimes. Not for always. Just sometimes.
Little Tommy Tucker All I do is sing for my supper. That's child's play. I'd like a challenge. An adventure.
Little Miss Muffet And I'm tired of being terrified by fierce spiders which nobody really believes I see anyway.
Little Jack Horner In short, Mother Goose, we're bored. Bored with being "Little" people of "little" consequence.

Pause

Mother Goose (*having an idea*) I tell you what. I was wondering what I could give you all as a Christmas present. And now I know. I'll think up a brand new nursery rhyme story with all of you in it.

The Children look interested

An adventure story. Excitement. Danger. A story in which each one of you does great things, each one of you has his or her big moment. How about it?
Children Yes, please; thank you, Mother Goose; how does it start?; let's hear it now; etc.

Mother Goose (*laughing*) Hold on. Quiet! Give me a chance to cogitate. (*She has an idea*) Magic. Every good story needs a bit of magic. Where can we find some magic?

They all wait a moment—to allow the audience to come up with the solution if they want to

Little Polly Flinders (*whispering, pointing to the decorations box*) Fairy Lethargia.

Mother Goose Of course. Lethargia. We'd better wake her up. She can do something useful for once. One, two, three.

All (*calling*) Fairy Lethargia.

Fairy Lethargia (*crawling from the box*) What is it now? (*She yawns*)

Little Miss Muffet Will you come and be in our story?

Fairy Lethargia No, I'm too tired for stories.

Little Bo Peep Please. All we want is some of your magic.

Fairy Lethargia (*indignantly*) What?

Little Jack Horner Just a little.

Little Tommy Tucker To make it a really special story.

Fairy Lethargia (*flattered*) Oh, very well. If it's a special story, count me in. Let's see. (*She collects her wand from the tree and waves it*)

To make your story special, to give it extra zip,
Three magic spells I'll let you have, and now I'll have a kip.

She replaces the wand and, yawning, returns to the decorations box

Mother Goose Thank you, Fairy Lethargia. Three spells. Mmm. We must only use them for emergencies and crisisisises. Now, gather round, little ones ... I'm sorry, gather round, everybody, and I'll begin the story. Now, let's see.

Music, as the Children listen to Mother Goose improvising the story. A lighting change here—narrowing to the "family" group—would help the atmosphere

Once upon a time, not very far away from here, at the other side of the forest, loomed a vast, mysterious, impenetrable stone castle. It was surrounded by a deep, inky-black moat in which lived a savage Monster who kept guard over the owner of the castle—the terrifying Giant Bossyboots. The Giant had only one interest in life—gold. Not that he had any, but he dreamed of possessing more gold than anyone else on earth. So he consulted all the old tomes about alchemy, trying to discover the secret of how to make gold. Then one day, as Mother Goose and her nursery rhyme children were sitting down to breakfast ...

From now on, the story takes over. The Lighting changes and the music continues

The Goose enters, perhaps in a follow spot. The Goose is tired and frightened. With wings flapping she breathes heavily to suggest she has been running or flying. She takes a short rest, looking off stage to check she is not being followed. Suddenly she sees the Book, rushes to it, searches till she finds the bellrope and pulls it

Inside, the Children and Mother Goose react to the bell. This is really a two-level reaction—in one sense it's a natural reaction to hearing a doorbell, and in another sense it is excited anticipation, because the Children know this is part of Mother Goose's story

Little Bo Peep Maybe my sheep have come home!

They jump up; dash to the door, open it and cluster round the Goose, leading it, confused by all the fuss, downstage. Mother Goose watches, not getting too involved; she wants the Children to experience the excitement of this new story

Little Miss Muffet Hallo, who are you?
Little Jack Horner It's a duck! Hallo, ducky!
Little Bo Peep No, it's not a duck. It's a goose. You're ignorant.
Little Jack Horner Not as ignorant as your sheep. Baaaaah!

Little Bo Peep bursts into tears again. The Goose reacts frightened, flapping its wings

Little Tommy Tucker It's all right. Don't get in a flap. We're not going to hurt you.
Little Miss Muffet Who are you? Where have you come from?

Little Polly Flinders suddenly comes into her own, almost taking herself by surprise

Little Polly Flinders Quiet! Sorry, but I think the Goose is frightened. (*To the Goose*) It's all right; you can tell us.

The Goose points to her beak and shakes her head

What's the matter?

The audience will possibly shout out that the Goose cannot speak

You *can't* tell us? Oh, you can't speak?

The Goose nods

Well, that doesn't matter. You can show us what you're trying to say and we'll all guess. (*Taking in the audience*) Won't we? Now, are you lost?

The Goose nods, then points off

Little Jack Horner She's pointing to the forest.

The Goose indicates "beyond the forest"

Little Polly Flinders What? Through the forest? The other side of the forest?

The Goose nods

(*Asking the others*) What's the other side of the forest?

The audience may shout out "The Giant's Castle". If not, Little Polly Flinders gets the answer herself—or from one of the others

The Giant's Castle?

The Goose nods nervously

Little Tommy Tucker You want to go to the Giant's Castle?

The Goose immediately flaps her wings in panic, and shakes her head

Little Polly Flinders No? What then?

The audience may suggest that the Goose has come from the Giant's Castle

  Oh. You've *come* from the Giant's Castle? Through the forest?

The Goose nods

Little Bo Peep You didn't see any lost sheep, did you?

The Goose shakes her head

The Others Shhh. Bo Peep, shut up, etc.
Little Polly Flinders What were you doing in the Castle?

The Goose does a Marcel Marceau-type mime, using her hands/wings to suggest being locked in—showing imaginary walls

Little Jack Horner Playing Blind Man's Buff?
Little Miss Muffet Looking for a secret panel?

The Goose shakes her head at each of these suggestions. The audience may help

Little Polly Flinders You were locked in?

The Goose nods

Little Miss Muffet In a dungeon?

The Goose shakes her head and mimes pacing up and down. Again, the audience should help

Little Polly Flinders In a cage?

The Goose nods

  What were you doing in the cage?

The Goose mimes laying eggs: sitting down then up. The audience are encouraged to help again

Little Jack Horner Sitting in a hot bath?
Little Polly Flinders No. Laying eggs?

The Goose nods

  And why should the Giant lock you in a cage laying eggs?

The audience should be encouraged to reach the answer, using the following logical stages. If required, Little Polly Flinders can find the solution herself:

(1) What does the Giant desire most? Gold.
(2) What could eggs have to do with gold? They could be golden eggs.

(3) Perhaps the Giant thought that this goose was the Goose that laid the
Golden Egg?

(4) Therefore he locked her in a cage, so that she couldn't escape, in the
hope that she'd eventually lay a golden egg.

But you never laid a Golden Egg?

The Goose shakes her head

So you escaped. And now you're homeless?

The Goose nods

Little Miss Muffet You can live with us if you like, can't she, Mother Goose?

Mother Goose "re-enters" the scene

Mother Goose Well ...

All look at her, pleading

With a name like mine, how can I refuse?

The Goose reacts happily. All cheer

What's your name, Goosey?

The Goose shrugs her shoulders

That's a funny name.

The audience may shout out that she has not got a name

You haven't got a name?

The Goose shakes her head

Well, that's terrible. We can't adopt you if we don't know what to call you.
What are we to do?

Little Tommy Tucker Let's think of a good goosey name for her.

Mother Goose Good idea, Tommy. Any ideas?

The children cannot think of anything

No? (*To the audience*) Can *anyone* think of a good goosey name?

*The audience shout out ideas, some of which are put to the Goose, who selects
one—a different name each performance. In the script let us call her Gertie*

Gertie? She likes Gertie? I know. Tommy. Sing a song for her.

Little Tommy Tucker All right. It'll make a change from singing for my
supper!

SONG 3: **The Song Of The Goose** (*Part 1*)

Little Tommy Tucker   Gertie!
                                You needn't flap
                                Gertie!
                                Don't fly away
                                Gertie!

>We'll take you under our wing
>So
>Gertie!
>Please stay.

Hey, I've got an idea. Why doesn't everyone (*taking in the audience*) join in whenever I sing the word Gertie? Would you do that? Then Gertie will see how many friends she's got to protect her from the Giant.

Little Bo Peep Shall I give a signal with my crook?—Every time I lift it like this, we all shout "GERTIE". All right? Let's have a practice. (*She raises her crook*)

All (*including the audience*) Gertie!

Little Bo Peep And again. (*She raises her crook*)

All (*including the audience*) Gertie!

Little Bo Peep Lovely!

SONG 3: **The Song Of The Goose** (*Part 2*)

All (*with audience*)	Gertie!
Little Tommy Tucker	You needn't flap
All (*with audience*)	Gertie!
Little Tommy Tucker	Don't fly away
All (*with audience*)	Gertie!
Little Tommy Tucker	We'll take you under our wing So
All (*with audience*)	Gertie!
Little Tommy Tucker	Please stay.
All	Who escaped from the Castle?
All (*with audience*)	Gertie!
All	Who escaped from the cage?
All (*with audience*)	Gertie!
All	Who escaped from the Giant?
All (*with audience*)	Gertie!
All	And left him in a rage? Well it was

Optional Chorus

All (*with audience*)	Gertie!
All	You needn't flap
All (*with audience*)	Gertie!
All	Don't fly away
All (*with audience*)	Gertie!
All	We'll take you under our wing So
All (*with audience*)	Gertie!
All	Please stay, Yes, it was

Final Chorus

All (*with audience*)	Gertie!
All	You needn't flap

All (*with audience*)	Gertie!
All	Don't fly away
All (*with audience*)	Gertie!
All	We'll take you under our wing
	So
All (*with audience*)	Gertie!
All	Please stay.
All (*with audience*)	Gertie!

During the song the Goose gets happier and happier, dancing energetically

Mother Goose Well done, everybody. Now, come on all of you. Jobs. Jack—you can make the beds. Polly—washing up. I need someone to help me make the figgy pudding.

Little Tommy Tucker I will!

Mother Goose All right. But fingers off my figgies. And someone to search for some holly to decorate the Book. Bo-Peep?

Little Bo Peep I'd rather stay here in case my sheep come home.

Little Miss Muffet I'll go holly-hunting. Gertie can come too.

Gertie nods

Mother Goose Don't be long. (*She gives Little Miss Muffet a basket*)

Little Miss Muffet (*as she and Gertie set off*) No. It's not far to the forest. There's lots of holly there.

Gertie stops abruptly at the mention of the word "forest". She trembles. Music echoes the danger

What's the matter, Gertie? The forest? Don't worry. (*Indicating the audience*) We'll make sure you're safe, won't we?

All Yes.

Little Miss Muffet 'Bye.

Music

   Little Miss Muffet and Gertie set off, perhaps through the auditorium, towards the forest

The others wave

The Others 'Bye.

Mother Goose Come on, children, to work.

They all revolve the Book back to its original position; then they enter the Book. Meanwhile, and after they are all in, the scene change takes place. If this needs a few extra seconds, it may be an idea to have a follow spot on Little Miss Muffet and Gertie as they progress through the auditorium, waving to the audience

SCENE 2

The Forest/Spider's Lair

This set should not be too complex. It could consist of several cut-out trees and/or borders, if possible reminiscent of a potentially sinister Arthur Rackham-style forest. Intertwining branches, interesting shapes. Incorporated into this is a holly bush or two, plus a raised "Tuffet" in front of the Spider's Lair—this could be a gnarled old tree trunk: but it should not be designed in such a way that the audience will spot straight away that something nasty is going to pop out—the entrance of the Spider should be a surprise

Sinister music as the lighting comes up on the rather spooky forest. Dramatic shadows made by the trees: perhaps some sinister noises—an owl hooting, a bat screeching

The Big Bad Wolf enters, sniffing the ground ahead of him, searching for tracks. He moves stealthily, stopping every few steps and sniffing—using his nose like a metal detector. Suddenly he finds a scent

Big Bad Wolf Aha ... (*He scurries along, following it, head down, body bent over. After a few paces he bangs straight into a tree trunk*) Ow! (*A sound like a wolf's howl. He rubs his head*) I don't like this creepy forest. I'm going home. (*He stands upright, banging his head on an overhead branch*) Ow! (*A bigger howl. He rubs his head*) Oh. I can feel one of my turns coming on. Tranquillizer, quick. (*He fumbles for a very large bottle of pills*) Oh, my nerves, my nerves they're in tags and ratters, raggers and tatty, tatties and rags, oh, they're in shreds, they really are. (*He pops a huge gob-stopper pill in his mouth. With his mouth full*) That's bett ... (*Suddenly he sees the audience. He reacts with violent surprise, spitting out the pill, and half-retreating behind the tree. To the audience*) Wh-wh-who are you? D-don't answer. I d-d-don't want to know. You didn't see that, do you understand, me t-taking that t-t-tranquillizer. I didn't take it. 'Cos I don't need t-t-tranquillizers. I'm f-f-fearless, n-nerveless, n-nothing frightens me. I'm the B-b-big, B-b-bad, W-w-wolf. No kid. And I'm strong, buff as old toots, I mean t-tough as old boots. So there. Ya boo! And that reminds me. Boo. I mean, that's what I'm here for. Looking, for a boo. Boo? Boo who? No, not boo-hoo, I mean, not looking for a boo, I mean looking for who you shouldn't say boo—to. Oh dear. (*He has an idea*) Maybe you could help. You see, I jerk for the Wyant, I mean work for the Giant in the castle, and he has a sweet little pet, a snowy-white Goose we all love, and who loves us too. But today, horror of horrors, she's esca ... she's disappeared, lost without trace, and the Giant is in tears, he's so worried about what awful fate may have befallen his little feathered friend. Now, all you kind animal lovers, hear my plea for a dumb creature in danger—and tell me, have you seen the Giant's Goose?

The audience should shout out "no"—they will realize the Big Bad Wolf is up to no good

Are you sure?
Audience Yes.

Big Bad Wolf Thank you. In that case I'd better go on searching. (*He puts his head down and starts sniffing again. Calling*) Goosey, Goosey, Goosey. (*He starts to exit*)

   The Bigger Badder Wolf enters suddenly

The Big Bad Wolf bumps into him, and jumps

   Ooh! Oh, it's you. (*He takes out another tranquillizer, and pops it in his mouth—in fact "palming" it*)

Bigger Badder Wolf Of course it's me. Pull yourself together. And stop taking those tranquillizers.

He bangs the Big Bad Wolf on the back, but instead of making him spit it out, it in fact makes him swallow it. He reacts wide-eyed

   Have you found the Goose?

Big Bad Wolf N-n-no. I was just asking these kind people ...

Bigger Badder Wolf Yes, I heard. Huh. (*He turns on the audience*) Now listen, you lot. I don't know who you are or why you're here, but something tells me you're all lying through your well-brushed teeth. You may think you can bamboozle the Big Bad Wolf with your devious tricks, but (*he cackles evilly*) I'm the *Bigger Badder* Wolf and no one, but no one, fools me.

Big Bad Wolf Hear, hear.

Bigger Badder Wolf I am the greatest.

Big Bad Wolf Hear, hear. And I am the second greatest.

Bigger Badder Wolf Hear, hear.

Big Bad Wolf
Bigger Badder Wolf } And nobody stands in our way. Hear, hear. { *speaking together*

Both confidently turn inwards as though to move off, and bump into each other. Both jump and scream. The Big Bad Wolf reacts nervously, the Bigger Badder Wolf reacts angrily

SONG 4: **With A Huff And A Puff**

The "huh, huh" noise suggested is a combination of exhaled breath and a sinister laugh

The Wolves	Huh huh huh huh huh huh huh
	With a huff and a puff
	We're rough and we're tough
	If you're climbing a tree, then
	We'll knock down your ladder;
	To make you feel sad
	Will make us feel glad
Big Bad Wolf	'Cos I'm big and bad
Bigger Badder Wolf	He's big and bad
	And I
Both	Huh huh huh huh huh
Bigger Badder Wolf	Am badder and bigger!
Both	Huh huh huh huh huh huh huh
	With a huff and a puff
	We're rough and we're tough

And we do dirty deeds for
A reas'nable figure,
And if people twig
We don't care a fig

Big Bad Wolf 'Cos I'm bad and big
Bigger Badder Wolf He's bad and big
And I

Both Huh huh huh huh huh
Bigger Badder Wolf Am bigger and badder!

Both If you're on your way home
On your own in the night
We'll be waiting in lurk
To give you a fright.
Huh huh huh huh huh huh huh
We'll creep up behind,
Then one leap in the dark
And you'll find
That our bite is far worse than our bark.

Huh huh huh huh huh huh huh
With a huff and a puff
We're rough and we're tough
We would rob our old granny
And not reimburse 'er;
It's not just a fad—
We've *always* been mad!—

Big Bad Wolf 'Cos I'm big and bad
Bigger Badder Wolf He's big and bad
And I

Both Huh huh huh huh huh
Bigger Badder Wolf Am bigger and worser!

Both So watch out and don't cross our path
It's years since we last had a bath
Yes, we're dirty and vicious
And highly suspicious
With venom as vile as an adder—
Two wolves at the door
Means trouble in store,
One big and bad
And one
Huh huh huh huh huh
Bigger and badder!

Huh huh huh huh huh huh huh
Huh!

At the end of the song, the music continues

*The Big Bad Wolf and the Bigger Badder Wolf exit downstage, one each side,
sniffing for the Goose's tracks. The Big Bad Wolf exits L, the Bigger Badder
Wolf exits R*

Simultaneously, from up R, Little Miss Muffet and Gertie enter, collecting holly in their basket

The music continues. They are unaware of any danger, in spite of possible audience reaction. They advance down L to another holly bush

The Big Bad Wolf, nose to the ground, enters up L and starts to cross the stage

The audience shout a warning, whereupon Gertie turns and sees the Big Bad Wolf. She gets in a flap, and desperately tries to mime to Little Miss Muffet that they are in danger

In the nick of time, sizing up the situation, Little Miss Muffet pulls Gertie off down L: in their panic they both drop their holly

At the same time, the Big Bad Wolf picks up the Goose's scent up RC and triumphantly follows it downstage. The music stops

Big Bad Wolf She's near. She's near. I can smack her trells—smell her tracks. Oh! Goosey, Goosey, Goosey! (*To the audience*) I'm getting warm, aren't I?

Audience No.

Big Bad Wolf Oh, yes I am.

Audience Oh, no you're not.

Big Bad Wolf Oh, yes I am.

Audience Oh, no you're not.

Big Bad Wolf Oooooh—no I'm not. (*Sniffing*) I've lost the scent again. Grrrr. Now listen, *please*, please help me or I'll get into trouble with the Bigger Badder Wolf. Which way did she go, eh? Did she go that way? (*He points off R*)

Audience (*lying*) Yes.

Big Bad Wolf (*pointing off L*) This way?

Audience No.

Big Bad Wolf (*pointing off R*) That way?

Audience Yes.

Big Bad Wolf You're sure?

Audience Yes.

Big Bad Wolf You're not having me on?

Audience No.

Big Bad Wolf Thank you. (*He starts to exit down R*)

The Bigger Badder Wolf enters suddenly down R

The Big Bad Wolf bumps into him, and jumps with fright

Bigger Badder Wolf You useless, wittering, witless wolf. You're not the second greatest, not the third greatest, you're the three thousand, two hundred and forty-fourth greatest. Just. And (*to the audience*) as for you lot—I was watching all the time. You're nothing but a mass of mamby-pamby flamboyantly fickle, feckless fibbers. The Goose went *that* way, and she had a girl with her and they were collecting holly.

Big Bad Wolf Golly.

Bigger Badder Wolf No, holly.

Big Bad Wolf Ooh, you rotten lot. I trusted you.

Bigger Badder Wolf Ha, ha, ha. Try fooling someone your own size next time. You can't fool the greatest.

Big Bad Wolf And you can't fool the three thousand, two hundred and forty-fourth greatest. Just. Not a second time, anyway.

Bigger Badder Wolf (*To the audience*) So, watch out.

Big Bad Wolf (*taking his pocket-watch out*) Half-past eleven.

Bigger Badder Wolf What?

Big Bad Wolf Half-past eleven. You said "watch out".

Bigger Badder Wolf (*hitting him*) Idiot. Come on.

They start to exit

(*To the audience*) Watch your step.

Big Bad Wolf (*watching his feet*) If I watch my step, I can't see where I'm going. (*He bumps into the Bigger Badder Wolf*)

Bigger Badder Wolf Oh, for wickedness sake . . . (*Hitting him*). I'm telling *them* to watch *their* step.

They start to move off

Big Bad Wolf Ah. Yes. (*To the audience, as evilly as he can*) Tread very, very carefully, or you'll put your foot in it.

They growl—then both howl (OW!): they have each put their foot in the holly dropped by Gertie and Little Miss Muffet. If possible, we can see it sticking to their feet. Then they overbalance and sit in the holly

Eventually the Big Bad Wolf and Bigger Badder Wolf run off screaming and shaking their paws in revenge at the audience.
Immediately, from up L, Little Miss Muffet and Gertie enter nervously: they edge down C, then across R, looking warily about them.
The two Wolves enter up L on tiptoe

The Wolves spot Little Miss Muffet and Gertie and, trying to "shush" the audience, advance upon them. Hearing the audience's warning, Little Miss Muffet and Gertie see the Wolves and a short chase starts—possibly through the auditorium and back on to the stage. N.B. This chase should not be too long or involved. Back on stage, all chase round a tree

After one revolution of the tree, Little Miss Muffet and Gertie escape off R

The Wolves are left chasing each other round the tree. Eventually they bump into each other and fall over

Furious, the Wolves look wildly about them, then exit down L. Immediately, Little Miss Muffet and Gertie enter up R and dash down C

Little Miss Muffet Quick, Gertie, run home to the Book.

Gertie wavers

Don't worry about me. I'll see you later.

Gertie speeds off down R

Little Miss Muffet, out of breath, sits down on the tuffet, and brings her curds and whey out of her basket. She begins to tuck in, hungrily and nervously

Suddenly, to sinister music, as from his lair, the large, furry frightening Spider enters slowly. He sees Little Miss Muffet, exults, and advances towards her

The audience scream a warning. The Spider arrives beside Little Miss Muffet. Sensing danger she slowly turns her head—in the wrong direction. Her head comes forward again; the Spider crosses behind her to the other side. She looks round again—in the other direction, thus missing the Spider again. Her head comes forward. She cannot understand the audience's concern. The Spider sits down beside her. Suddenly she "feels" his presence and with a slow burn, turns her head to face him. She sees him and screams. She leaps up and runs in a panic down R, then turns and runs across towards down L

Meanwhile, the Spider retreats back into his lair, and the Wolves enter suddenly down L

Little Miss Muffet runs straight into the arms of the Wolves. They hold on to her firmly

Bigger Badder Wolf Got you. Ha, ha, ha. Now, little girl, where is she, eh?
Big Bad Wolf Where's Goosey Goosey?
Little Miss Muffet I don't know. Let me go, you're hurting.
Bigger Badder Wolf Not until you help us find that scraggy bird.

Suddenly there is a dramatic Lighting change. Everything is black but for a small spotlight on Little Miss Muffet's face. The action freezes

SONG 5: **My Big Moment**

Little Miss Muffet   This must be my big moment
                              My moment of glory
                              In the story
                              This will be my closest shave
                              This must be my big moment
                              This is my time to be brave.

At the end of the song the Lights return to normal and the action starts again, the Wolves hanging on to the struggling Little Miss Muffet

All right, all right. I'll tell you. I'll tell you all I know.
Bigger Badder Wolf Sensible. Right, where is she?
Big Bad Wolf Where's Goosey Goosey?
Little Miss Muffet But only if you stop hurting my arms.
Bigger Badder Wolf All right.

They release their grip

Now, where is she?
Little Miss Muffet Come and sit down and I'll tell you.

She sits to one side of the tuffet. The Big Bad Wolf moves towards her

Bigger Badder Wolf Stop. (*To Little Miss Muffet*) No trickery now.

Little Miss Muffet Of course not. (*Sweetly*) How could I ever trick two such clever wolves as you?

Big Bad Wolf (*flattered*) Hey, she's right, B.B.W. We're the greatest.

Bigger Badder Wolf Well, all right. But we've got our eyes on you.

They sit down on the tuffet, the Big Bad Wolf next to Little Miss Muffet, and the Bigger Badder Wolf next to him

Little Miss Muffet Are you hungry?

Big Bad Wolf Starving. Didn't have any breakfast.

Little Miss Muffet You can share my elevenses if you like. (*She offers her curds and whey*)

Big Bad Wolf Ooh, thanks. What is it?

Little Miss Muffet Curds and whey.

Big Bad Wolf Ughhh. Sounds horrible.

Little Miss Muffet Try some.

Bigger Badder Wolf Hold it. (*He sniffs the bowl*) Could be poison.

Little Miss Muffet Don't be silly. (*She takes some on her finger and eats it*)

Big Bad Wolf Yes. Don't be silly, B.B.W. (*He takes a spoonful*) Mmm. Very tasty. Try some.

The Bigger Badder Wolf, after a moment's hesitation, tries some

Bigger Badder Wolf Mmmmm.

Little Miss Muffet, in preparation for what is to happen, shuts her eyes tight

Music as the Spider emerges stealthily from his lair, and advances upon the Wolves

The Bigger Badder Wolf is holding the bowl, tucking in greedily. The Spider, in pantomime fashion, taps the Bigger Badder Wolf on the shoulder. He thinks it is the Big Bad Wolf

Get off.

Big Bad Wolf What?

Bigger Badder Wolf You've had your turn. Don't be greedy.

The Spider again taps the Bigger Badder Wolf on the shoulder

I said get off.

Big Bad Wolf I don't know what you're talking about.

The Spider sits down beside the Big Bad Wolf

Bigger Badder Wolf Stop bashing me.

Big Bad Wolf I didn't bash you. (*Turning to the Spider*) Did I?

The Spider shakes his head. The Big Bad Wolf's head returns front

No. Cheek. I never touched you.

The Big Bad Wolf does an enormous double take, sees the Spider again, and, terrified, exits

The Bigger Badder Wolf, who is still tucking in, does not see the Big Bad Wolf go. The Spider moves along the tuffet, bringing himself next to the Bigger Bad Wolf. He digs him in the ribs

Bigger Badder Wolf I've told you, don't do that. You've had your share.

The Spider taps his knee

And don't tickle my leg either.

The Spider does it again

I'm warning you ...

The Bigger Badder Wolf taps the spider's "knee". The Spider shakes with laughter. The Bigger Badder Wolf suddenly does a double "thinks" look, and gingerly reaches out and touches the Spider's knee—it clearly does not feel like the Big Bad Wolf's knee. He runs his hand up and down the Spider's leg/legs, gradually getting panic-stricken

   Finally the Bigger Badder Wolf looks round, sees the Spider, screams and dashes off, throwing down the bowl and spoon

Hearing the scream, Little Miss Muffet opens her eyes and, summoning up all her courage, turns to see the Spider. The Spider cheekily and endearingly waves a leg or two. Little Miss Muffet tentatively waves back, then stretches across and shakes hands with the Spider. They share a moment of triumph over the Wolves. She gives him a kiss and waves good-bye. He waves back with all his legs

   Little Miss Muffet exits towards home, i.e. down R

The Spider picks up the bowl of curds and whey and starts to gobble it up. The lights fade

Scene 3

Back at the Book

Music. Mother Goose, Little Jack Horner, Little Tommy Tucker, Little Bo Peep and Little Polly Flinders enter

During the song they could well be effecting the scene change back to the Book, revolving it to display the inside, then decorating it, etc., and preparing the table and props for the cookery scene that follows

SONG 6: **Getting Ready For Christmas.**

Mother Goose
Little Jack Horner
Little Bo Peep   *(singing)*
Little Tommy Tucker
Little Polly Flinders

       We're getting ready for Christmas
       We're getting ready for Christmas Day

Building a snowman
From cotton-wool snow
Hanging up the holly
And the mistletoe
We're getting ready
Getting ready for Christmas
Ready,
Steady—

We're getting ready for Christmas
We're getting ready for Christmas Day
Filling the stockings
As full as can be
Wrapping up the presents
For the Christmas tree
We're getting ready
Getting ready for Christmas
Ready,
Steady—

It's nearly time for the celebrations
Fun and festivity lie in store
It's time to put up the decorations
With a welcoming Christmas wreath upon the door.
We're getting ready for Christmas
We're getting ready for Christmas Day
Roasting the chestnuts
And chopping the wood
Blowing up balloons and
Helping stir the pud
We're getting ready
Getting ready for Christmas
Ready,
Steady—
Go!

Suggested instrumental verse for dance

We're getting ready for Christmas
We're getting ready for Christmas Day
Shining a candle
From each window pane
Making paper hats and
Miles of paper chain
We're getting ready
Getting ready for Christmas
Ready
Steady—

It's nearly time for the celebrations
Fun and festivity lie in store

It's time to put up the decorations
With a welcoming Christmas wreath upon the door.

We're getting ready for Christmas
We're getting ready for Christmas Day
Stuffing the turkey
And scrubbing the floors
Sweeping out the chimney
For old Santa Claus
We're getting ready
Getting ready for Christmas
Ready
Steady—
Go, go, go—
Christmas
Hallo.

Little Jack Horner, Little Bo Peep and Little Polly Flinders exit to do more decorating on the "outside" of the Book

Mother Goose and Little Tommy Tucker remain behind to prepare the figgy pudding. The following slapstick-style scene could be embellished further into a "speciality" if it is felt that not enough scope is given here: but it should not last too long, as, however funny it may be, it does hold up the plot

Mother Goose (*putting on an overall and chef's hat*) Now, Tommy, time to make the figgy pudding.
Little Tommy Tucker (*singing*) Now bring me some figgy pudding,
                                        Now bring me ...
Mother Goose Yes, all right dear. Be a good boy and fetch me the dough.
Little Tommy Tucker Dough?
Mother Goose Dough. D.O. Dough.
Little Tommy Tucker Oh. Dough. Right ho. (*He goes to the back of the set, singing as he works*) Do, ray, me, fah, so, la, te (*coming forward with the tray of dough*) DO!
Mother Goose (*busy doing something else, e.g. weighing out currants, so not looking*) Hurry up, dear.

Little Tommy Tucker staggers under the weight of the dough, and puts it down, on the floor in front of the table. He has to crouch to do this, so is temporarily out of Mother Goose's vision

(*Looking up and not seeing him*) Tommy!

Little Tommy Tucker stands up. She sees him

Stop playing, dear (*coming round to the front of the table*) and (*one step per word*) go-fetch-the-dough. (*On the word "dough" she steps in the dough*) Ohhhh!

Together they pull it off her boot

Little Tommy Tucker Oh. You've put your foot in it!

Mother Goose Now, concentrate, Tommy. (*Returning behind the table*) Place
the dough *here*. (*Patting the end of the table, then returning to counting her
currants*)

*Little Tommy Tucker struggles with the dough, which should be rather pliable
and elastic*

Here. (*She gives another pat*)

*Little Tommy Tucker manages to put the dough down where Mother Goose
wants it*

Here. (*This time her hand crashes into the dough*) Ughhhh!
Little Tommy Tucker You've put your hand in it now.
Mother Goose Tommy, a little con-cen-tra-tion if you please.
Little Tommy Tucker Con-cen-tra-tion.

*Mother Goose kneads the dough into a large ball. A rolling-pin is visible on the
table*

Mother Goose Take the dough (*she hands it to him*) and roll it.
Little Tommy Tucker Eh?
Mother Goose (*back with her currants*) Roll it. Hurry up.

*Little Tommy Tucker shrugs his shoulders and rolls the ball of dough along the
floor*

Little Tommy Tucker Wheeee!
Mother Goose (*seeing this*) No, no, no, Tommy. Use the rolling-pin. (*She
hands him the rolling pin*) This. (*She returns to her currants*)

*Little Tommy Tucker takes the rolling-pin, and after a moment's hesitation, uses
it as a bat to roll the dough further along the floor*

(*Seeing this*) No, no, no, Tommy. (*Deliberately*) Roll it with the rolling-
pin, thus. (*She mimes the movement*)
Little Tommy Tucker (*echoing the movement*) Thus.
Mother Goose Thus.
Little Tommy Tucker Thus.

*It now becomes a rhythmic movement, complete with knees bend, etc. Both
enjoy it*

Mother Goose Thus.
Little Tommy Tucker Thus.

As they continue, Mother Goose gets carried away

Mother Goose (*suddenly*) Stop it! Now get on with it, Tommy, and con-cen-
trate.

*Little Tommy Tucker mouths the word "con-cen-trate" with her. He starts roll-
ing the dough correctly, except that he is still doing it on the floor*

(*Seeing this*) No, no, no, Tommy. Not on the floor. On the table. On the
table.

Little Tommy Tucker immediately jumps on the table, giving Mother Goose a fright

Aaaaah! Not you, the dough.

Little Tommy Tucker Oh. (*He collects the dough, puts it on the table and starts rolling it with the rolling-pin. If possible, as the dough gets flatter and bigger, it spreads on to Mother Goose's outstretched hand and arm, so that they get rolled too. In rolling rhythm*) Thus. Thus. Thus.

He eventually notices the bump, investigates, and, looking for where the bump leads, traces it up the arm to find Mother Goose's long-suffering face staring at him. She slowly lifts her hand, letting the dough hang

Mother Goose ⎱
Little Tommy Tucker ⎰ Con-cen-trate. ⎰ (*speaking*
                                            ⎱ *together*)
Mother Goose Now, fetch the baking tin.

Little Tommy Tucker goes to the back of the set. Mother Goose scatters the currants over the dough and wraps it over, "folding in the ends". Little Tommy Tucker brings forward a tin, then suddenly screams, and drops the tin like a hot brick, with a clatter

Mother Goose (*with a jump*) What was that?
Little Tommy Tucker The baking tin. It's baking! Tara!
Mother Goose (*dividing the dough in two*) Don't be silly. Now, we'll make one family-size figgy pudding (*she places half the dough in the tin, and scatters dusting powder on it*) and a dozen small ones. (*She starts dividing the other half into smaller tennis-ball-size sections*)

Suddenly Little Tommy Tucker's attention is drawn to the baking tin, where the pudding is "rising" rapidly. In fact this is done with a balloon blowing up beneath the dough. N.B. This may have to be in a different tin, switched for the original one. This could have a thin layer of dough over the balloon, which pushes it up when blown up. As the pudding gets bigger and bigger, Little Tommy Tucker grabs Mother Goose's attention. They both look at it, then Mother Goose prods it with a wooden spoon (with a pin attached). It bursts, spraying dough or dusting powder over their faces

Mother Goose Self-raising flour! (*Returning to the small ones*) Right, Tommy. Into the oven.

The oven could be "under the table" or in another part of the set. Tommy starts to get in it

Not you. The figgy puddings.

Tommy gets out of the oven. To music, Mother Goose starts throwing the balls of dough to Little Tommy Tucker, the idea being that he should transfer them to the oven. If the actor playing Little Tommy Tucker can juggle, he could go into a short routine here. Eventually, he has too many to hold and Mother Goose is throwing more, without looking at him

At this point Little Jack Horner, Little Bo Peep and Little Polly Flinders enter

Little Tommy Tucker throws the "balls" to them; they spread out and catch the "balls" in a circular chain. The last one returns the "balls" to the table, for Mother Goose to pick up and throw at Little Tommy Tucker again. She is unaware that this is going on, of course. The catching game, to music, continues for a short while. Then Mother Goose notices what is going on. Her immediate reaction is one of annoyance, but this changes to amusement and enjoyment. She suddenly picks up a frying pan or similar object and, as the "balls" come back to her, whacks them, cricket or tennis-style. The first few she hits stay on the stage. Then Little Tommy Tucker starts throwing into the "chain", "balls" from another source. These are cotton-wool balls, and are clouted fair and square by Mother Goose into the audience. N.B. This fairly traditionally panto routine could be omitted; the cookery scene could end on the line "Self-raising flour", at which point the others enter

Suddenly, as the fun with the audience is in full flood, Gertie enters from the forest and runs to the door and pulls the bell-rope

The "game" freezes at the sound of the bell

Little Bo Peep Is that my sheep?

Mother Goose No, it's Little Miss Muffet and Gertie back from holly hunting, I expect.

Little Jack Horner opens the door, in rushes Gertie in a flurry, flapping her wings. They all cluster round her

Little Jack Horner	What is it?
Little Tommy Tucker	What's the matter? etc. } *(speaking together)*
Little Bo Peep	What's happened, Gertie? etc.

Gertie is confused

Mother Goose Quiet. You can see she's in a state. Polly. Come and do your stuff.

Little Polly Flinders comes forward

Little Polly Flinders What is it, Gertie? Did you meet somebody?

Gertie nods, and does a wolf impersonation. The audience will probably help interpret

What? A monster? The Giant? A wolf?

Gertie nods, and mimes "two"

Two wolves?

Little Bo Peep *(freezing with terror)* Wolves?
Little Polly Flinders Did they chase you?

Gertie nods

Mother Goose Where's Little Miss Muffet?

Gertie mimes a boxing match

Little Polly Flinders She's fighting them?

Gertie nods

Mother Goose Ooh. (*She swallows hard*) I hope she's careful. (*Trying not to appear too worried*) She had a clean apron on this morning. (*She blinks away a tear*)

Little Tommy Tucker She'll be all right, Mother.

Little Bo Peep Wolves! (*She bursts into tears*)

Little Jack Horner Don't cry, Bo Peep; Little Miss Muffet will be back soon.

Little Bo Peep I'm not worried about her, I'm worried about my poor little sheep. Alone in the forest. Surrounded by wolves. Wolves like nothing better than sheep—to eat! I'll never see them again.

The others look at one another and shrug their shoulders, as she dashes out of the door, to "outside" the Book, which then revolves to reveal the outside cover again. Little Bo Peep looks out in all directions, hoping for a glimpse of her sheep

SONG 7: **Sheep, Sheep**

Little Bo Peep   Sheep, sheep
                             This is Bo Beep
                             Oh can you hear
                             What I say?
                             Or have you strayed
                             Too far?

                             Sheep, sheep
                             I'm losing sleep
                             Oh don't you know
                             How I care
                             Please tell me where
                             You are.

One by one, the others—Little Jack Horner, Little Tommy Tucker and Little Polly Flinders—put their heads over or round the Book

Little Jack Horner (*speaking*) Baaaaaaaa!
Little Tommy Tucker (*speaking*) Baaaaaaaa!
Little Polly Flinders (*speaking*) Baaaaaaaa!
All three (*speaking*) Baaaaaaaa!

Little Bo Peep swings round, thinking her sheep have been found. When she sees it is the others sending her up, she is cross, but tries to preserve her dignity

Little Bo Peep (*speaking*) Oh, it's you.

The other three sing with a sheep-like wobble in their voices

Little Polly Flinders ⎫
Little Tommy Tucker ⎬ (*singing together*)
Little Jack Horner   ⎭

Baaaaaa! Baaaaaa!
We've not strayed far
And we'll return
Very soon
This afternoon
You'll see.

Baaaaaa! Baaaaaa!
Daft things we are!
But if you leave
Us alone
We'll hurry home
For tea.

Little Bo Peep tries to take no notice

Little Bo Peep   Sheep, sheep
This is Bo Peep
Oh tell me why
Must you go?
Why are you so
Unkind?

Little Jack Horner ⎫
Little Tommy Tucker ⎬ *(singing together)*
Little Polly Flinders ⎭

Baaaaa! baaaaa!
Stupid we are
But we'll come back
Without fail
Bringing our tails
Behind.

Little Bo Peep   Sheep, sheep.

Little Jack Horner ⎫   ⎧
Little Tommy Tucker ⎬ Baaaaa! Baaaaa! ⎨ *(singing together)*
Little Polly Flinders ⎭   ⎩

*Dabbing her eyes, Little Bo Peep has a final look, shakes her head and goes
back in the Book*

Little Jack Horner ⎫   ⎧
Little Tommy Tucker ⎬ Baaaaaaaaaaaaa! ⎨ *(singing together)*
Little Polly Flinders ⎭   ⎩
Little Bo Peep   Sheep, sheep.

Their heads disappear from view

*Sinister chord as the Bigger Badder Wolf enters, rubbing his hands in glee; he
has seen Little Bo Peep go in. He is followed by the Big Bad Wolf, head down*

sniffing the tracks. The Bigger Badder Wolf stops. The Big Bad Wolf bumps into him. The Bigger Badder Wolf hits him

Big Bad Wolf Sorry, B.B.W. (*Nervously he takes out a tranquillizer*)
Bigger Badder Wolf (*imitating*) Sorry, B.B.W. (*Crossly*) And stop taking tranquillizers.

He knocks it out of the Big Bad Wolf's hand, making it bounce high in the air. The Bigger Badder Wolf catches it under his hat. Alternatively it is allowed to bounce out into the auditorium

Big Bad Wolf Sorry, B.B.W.
Bigger Badder Wolf And stop saying "Sorry, B.B.W." It gets on my nerves.
Big Bad Wolf Sorry, B.B.W. (*He realizes too late, and clamps his hand over his mouth*)
Bigger Badder Wolf Now, listen. Tracks end here, right?
Big Bad Wolf Right here, right.
Bigger Badder Wolf (*pointing to the Book*) Goose in there, therefore, right?
Big Bad Wolf Right there, therefore, right.
Bigger Badder Wolf Problem: to get inside, right? And not be left outside, right?
Big Bad Wolf Ah! Right. Not left outside, but right inside, right! Not outside left but inside right to centre forward and shoot and it's a goal! Hooray! (*He jumps up and down*)

The Bigger Badder Wolf clamps his hand over the Big Bad Wolf's mouth

Bigger Badder Wolf Shhh. Solution: take off your coat.
Big Bad Wolf What?
Bigger Badder Wolf Take off your coat.
Big Bad Wolf I'll catch cold.
Bigger Badder Wolf You'll catch more than a cold if you don't. Now (*Helping him out of his coat*) take it off and turn it inside out, right?
Big Bad Wolf Inside out, right. Not outside in, left. Inside out ...
Bigger Badder Wolf And don't start all that again.
Big Bad Wolf I didn't start it. You started it.

By this time, the Big Bad Wolf's coat is back on—inside out, revealing the thick sheepskin lining

Bigger Badder Wolf Now. Baaaa.
Big Bad Wolf I beg your pardon.
Bigger Badder Wolf Baaaa. Baaaaa! (*He encourages the Big Bad Wolf to copy the noise*)

The Big Bad Wolf has not a clue what he is on about

Big Bad Wolf Baaaa?
Bigger Badder Wolf (*nodding*) Baaaaa! (*Louder and more manic*) Baaaaaa!
Big Bad Wolf Do you want a tranquillizer?
Bigger Badder Wolf Oh, give me strength!
Big Bad Wolf No, but it'll calm you down.

Bigger Badder Wolf You baaaa.
Big Bad Wolf Me baaaa?
Bigger Badder Wolf Yes, you baaaa. Look, didn't you hear that girl bleating
on about her lost sheep?

The Big Bad Wolf nods

(*Slowly and clearly*) Well, *you* are now a wolf in sheep's clothing, right?
And that means ...

He is stopped by a shout off

Little Miss Muffet Mother Goose! Mother Goose!
Bigger Badder Wolf Look out!

*The Bigger Badder Wolf drags the Big Bad Wolf off to hide. They exit the side
opposite the one they entered—i.e. not the side established as leading to the forest.
Little Miss Muffet rushes on from the forest: she rings frantically on the bell*

Little Miss Muffet Mother Goose! Quick.

*The door opens and Mother Goose, Gertie and the four other Children emerge,
and cluster round her. Little Polly Flinders carries the kettle with her*

All She's back. Thank goodness you're safe. Are you all right? etc.
Little Miss Muffet (*breathlessly*) Wolves. After Gertie. From the Giant's
Castle. They're coming.
Little Bo Peep What are we going to do?
Little Jack Horner Shut ourselves in the Book.

All turn to go in the door

Little Miss Muffet No.

They stop

They're strong. They'll smash the door down if they know Gertie's inside.
(*She grabs Gertie*) I'll hide with her in the forest.
Little Polly Flinders Can I come?
Little Jack Horner And me.
Little Tommy Tucker Me too! I'll bring the figgy pud. All right, Mother
Goose?
Mother Goose I suppose so, dear. But do take care, all of you.

Little Tommy Tucker rushes in and collects some figgy pud

Little Bo Peep I'd better stay here, in case my sheep turn up. (*She starts sniffing*)
Mother Goose Very well, dear.
Little Miss Muffet Come on.

*Little Miss Muffet leads a nervous Gertie off. The others follow—they exit
towards the forest, Mother Goose waving*

Mother Goose I'll see you off.

*Mother Goose exits. Little Bo Peep goes back in the Book and shuts the door.
Immediately, music is heard as the Wolves enter from the other side*

The Bigger Badder Wolf pushes the disguised Big Bad Wolf to the door. The Big Bad Wolf rings the bell, then bends over to look more like a sheep

Big Bad Wolf Baaaaa! Baaaaaa!

The door opens

> *The Bigger Badder Wolf backs away to avoid being seen, and in fact exits on the forest side, looking eagerly towards the Book. This is to prevent the audience thinking he is chasing after the others.*

> *Little Bo Peep emerges*
> Baaaaaa!

Little Bo Peep (*yelling with delight*) Little sheep! You've come home!

She falls upon the "sheep", stroking and hugging him. By this time the audience may well be screaming a warning

> You're safe from the Wolves, now. Come in.

She takes him in and shuts the door behind them. Pause. Suddenly, a bloodcurdling scream is heard. The door opens again and Little Bo Peep, screaming, tries to get out, but each time is seen to be pulled roughly back inside. Growling noises from the Big Bad Wolf. But Little Bo Peep has her crook with her and manages to stave off the Wolf with it. N.B. It may be possible to work out a short routine using the crook as a catching device. Little Bo Peep could emerge from the door a couple of times, but be suddenly caught round the neck with the crook and hauled in again. Then the situations could be reversed, with Little Bo Peep catching the Big Bad Wolf by the neck trying to drag him inside so she can get out. Finally the door is shut, and we imagine the Big Bad Wolf is a little stunned inside. Little Bo Peep, screaming still, rushes down R, nearly exits, then, remembering that the others went in the other direction, turns round and starts to run off L

> *Mother Goose enters down L*

Little Bo Peep is stopped in her tracks

> Oh, Mother Goose, Mother Goose. (*She flings herself into Mother Goose's arms, pointing indoors to where the Big Bad Wolf is. Hysterically*) A wolf, a wolf. Rang the bell and I thought it was one of my sheep and let him in and ... ohhh! (*She sobs*)

Mother Goose There, there, dear. You're safe now. Stop crying.

The sobbing lessens with the reassuring pats on the back

Little Bo Peep I'm sorry. I can't help it. He was so horrible—and he's still in the Book!

Mother Goose There, there.

For the first time, Little Bo Peep looks up, through tear-stained eyes at Mother Goose

Little Bo Peep Oh, Mother Goose, how strong your arms are.

Mother Goose All the better to comfort you, my dear.

Music chord

Little Bo Peep Oh, Mother Goose. (*A little uncomfortable*) How big your eyes look today.
Mother Goose All the better to watch over you, my dear.

Music chord

Little Bo Peep (*nervously*) Oh, Mother Goose, how long and sharp your teeth look.
Mother Goose All the better to *bite* you with, my dear.

Music. Dramatic struggle, but not too long, in which "Mother Goose" is revealed to be the Bigger Badder Wolf in disguise—in fact wearing Mother Goose's dress. N.B. This revelation should, if possible, come as a real surprise to the audience. The tussle ends with the Big Bad Wolf entering from the Book, rubbing his head; he is finishing off writing a note, which he speedily attaches to the door. Then he helps subdue the struggling, screaming Little Bo Peep. They lift her up and tuck her under their arms. Suddenly the Lighting changes dramatically, to solely a follow-spot on Little Bo Peep. Simultaneously the action freezes

SONG 7A: **My Big Moment** (*reprise*)

Little Bo Peep (*singing*)   This must be my big moment
My moment of glory
In the story
This will be my closest shave
This must be my big moment
This is my time to be brave.

At the end of the song, the lighting reverts and the action starts again, and the growling Wolves carry off the struggling Little Bo Peep. They exit down L towards the forest. Simultaneously, Mother Goose enters up L, in her undies, still spinning from the shock of being attacked by the Bigger Badder Wolf

The audience may well shout out that Little Bo Peep has been caught, or that the Wolves have left a note. In any case, she staggers to the door, goes to open it, notices the note, rips it off the door and studies it

Mother Goose (*reading*) "We, the Wolves of the Giant's Castle, wish to inform Mother Goose that Little Bo Peep is in our clutches. If you ever want to set eyes on her again you must bring the Giant's Goose into the Forest within the hour and we will do a swap. The Goose for Little Bo Peep. Yours threateningly, The Big Bad Wolf and the Bigger Badder Wolf." Oh, no. What's to be done? (*Calling*) Children! (*Remembering*) they've all gone. Poor Little Bo Peep. Poor Gertie. Now calm down, Mother Goose, calm down, don't panic, don't panic, don't panic. (*Pause. She takes a deep breath to calm down. Suddenly she shouts*) HE——LP! Emergency, emergency. He——lp! (*She has an idea*) Fairy Lethargia, of course. (*To the audience*) Quick, let's wake her up. One, two, three.

Audience   ⎫
Mother Goose ⎬ Fairy Lethargia. ⎰ (*calling together*)

Mother Goose Once more. One, two, three.
Audience ⎱ Fairy Lethargia. ⎰ *(calling together)*
Mother Goose ⎰   ⎱

A yawning, stretching Fairy Lethargia eases her way out of the decorations box

Fairy Lethargia Cor dear, I'm up and down like a blinking yoyo ... oh. (*She sees the audience as she climbs out, puts on her act again*)

Hallo, hallo, it's Christmas Eve, and I'm your Christmas Fairy
My spells will get you out of spots and situations hairy ...

(*Suddenly she sees Mother Goose*) Ha, ha, ha, ha.

Moother Goose What's the matter?
Fairy Lethargia You look funny with your undies on.
Mother Goose I look funnier with them off.
Fairy Lethargia Ha, ha, ha, ha.
Mother Goose Stop laughing. This looks serious.
Fairy Lethargia It doesn't from where I'm standing. Ha, ha.
Mother Goose I've been hijacked by a wolf. And Little Bo Peep's been kidnapped. Wolfnapped. I need the first of our three spells, please.
Fairy Lethargia Oh.
Mother Goose Oh what?
Fairy Lethargia O.K. (*Taking the wand off the tree*) What's it to be?
Mother Goose Er. (*She thinks*) Miss Muffet and Polly and Tommy and Jack—oh, and Gertie—I need them here, so we can decide what to do.
Fairy Lethargia Where are they now?
Mother Goose If I knew that, I wouldn't ask for a spell to get them back, would I?
Fairy Lethargia All right, all right, don't get your knickers in a twist. (*She looks at Mother Goose's undies and giggles again*)
Mother Goose I'll go and find my dressing-gown.

Mother Goose goes in the door

Fairy Lethargia takes up a pose, holds up the wand, and starts the spell, accompanied by not-very-graceful movements

SONG 8: **Fairy Lethargia's Magic Spell**

Fairy Lethargia   Gertie and Little Miss Muffet
                                    And Tommy and Polly and Jack
                                    Abracadabra, hocus pocus
                                    Magic the lot of them back.

At the end of the spell, the four Children and Gertie return "by magic". This could be achieved by use of trap doors, flash boxes, a swift BLACK-OUT, etc. At any event, all five return, and are surprised to find themselves transported back to the Book. Little Tommy Tucker carries a substantially reduced figgy pudding; Little Polly Flinders carries her kettle

Fairy Lethargia curtsies to acknowledge possible audience applause—depending on how well the magical appearances were done!

Little Jack Horner (*waking up*) What's happened?

Fairy Lethargia Spell Number One's happened, that's what. Pretty spectacular, eh? (*She blows her fingernails, or does some other self-congratulatory movement*)

Little Tommy Tucker We're back.

Little Miss Muffet But why?

Mother Goose enters from the Book; she wears her dressing-gown

Mother Goose Oh, thank goodness. Well done, Lethargia. Have a rest, dear. Children, listen.

The Children and Gertie, still "waking up" gather round Mother Goose

Little Bo Peep has been wolfnapped. By the kids ... I mean, kidnapped by the Wolves.

This jerks them into life

Children What? How? Where have they taken her? etc.

Mother Goose Shhh. Listen. They left a note saying that if we ever want to see her again, we must meet them in the forest.

Gertie involuntarily flaps her wings

Then they will give us back Little Bo Peep on condition that we—that we—well, children, that we—in exchange as it were—give them back—(*She can hardly bring herself to say it*)—Gertie.

Music. Gertie slowly turns away from the group, and, head down, sadly waddles down-stage. She is obviously crying. N.B. This must not be overdone—it is a very tender moment. The others watch her

Gertie, dear. I wouldn't have had this happen for all the world, you know that, don't you?

Gertie nods

But what can I do? Eh? I must save Little Bo Peep. I'm sorry.

Gertie nods and, resigned, starts moving off towards the forest. The music builds as the others all set off too. A sad procession, which Fairy Lethargia joins. Little Polly Flinders still has her kettle. The Lights fade

Scene 4

The Forest—without the Spider's Lair

The music continues as the scene changes. The following sequence is all done in mime to music. If desirable, a forest front cloth could fly in to cover the scene change. The two snarling Wolves enter, carrying a distressed Little Bo Peep.

They pause for a few moments to shake their fists at the audience, who should be booing them. The Bigger Badder Wolf removes Mother Goose's dress, while the Big Bad Wolf retains a grip on Little Bo Peep. The dress is thrown roughly on the ground, and maybe stamped on. Then they exit, or, if a front cloth is not being used—it may be possible, for example, for them to enter through the auditorium and reach the stage just as the scene change has been effected, taking the dress off on the way—they hide behind a tree

The music continues, playing a sad version of the Goose's song, as Gertie, with the Children, Mother Goose and Fairy Lethargia, enter the forest. They, too, could come through the auditorium, or go across the front cloth, or simply arrive in the forest. They find Mother Goose's dress on the ground, and know they are on the right route. Mother Goose takes the dress with her. The Children surround Gertie protectively

Suddenly, the Wolves and Bo Peep emerge. The two sides confront each other. Little Bo Peep outstretches her arms for help. Mother Goose, firmly but sympathetically, forces the Children to let Gertie go. Each one kisses her good-bye. Mother Goose takes her by the wing and advances to "no-man's land" in the centre. The Wolves bring Little Bo Peep forward. The exchange is made. Little Bo Peep embraces Mother Goose, who leads her back to the "family"

Meanwhile, the Wolves grab Gertie and perhaps put a rope round her neck, before roughly forcing her to go with them towards the Giant's Castle. The others watch them disappear, with obviously conflicting emotions—relief for Little Bo Peep's safety and sadness at Gertie's disappearance.

The music stops

Little Bo Peep Where's Gertie going?

Mother Goose Back to the Giant's Castle. It was either her or you, dear.

Little Bo Peep But we can't just let her be locked up in a cage again. (*To the others*) Can we?

Little Miss Muffet She's right.

Little Tommy Tucker But what else can we do? Mother Goose?

Mother Goose It's up to you, children. Remember, this is *your* story, *your* adventure ...

Pause. Fairy Lethargia falls asleep on her feet

Little Jack Horner We'll rescue Gertie.

All Hear, hear; hooray, etc.

Little Polly Flinders (*plucking up courage*) And—and—and teach that stinking old Giant Bossyboots a lesson he'll never forget.

All Hear, hear; hooray, etc.

Mother Goose But don't forget it'll be dangerous—we'll have to face the forest and the castle and the Wolves and the Giant, not to mention the Monster of the Moat.

Little Tommy Tucker They'll help make it a real adventure.

Little Miss Muffet And we've still got two of Fairy Lethargia's spells left. Haven't we?

Lethargia is still asleep on her feet. All turn to see her. She snores

Little Bo Peep She's nodded off again.
Mother Goose Come on, then, everybody. One, two, three.
All Fairy Lethargia.
Fairy Lethargia (*suddenly waking with a start*) Ooh! (*Lifting her wand, and putting on her act*)

Hallo, hallo, 'tis Christmas Eve, and I'm ...

All (*shouting her down*) No! Quiet! Shh! etc.
Fairy Lethargia What's going on?

SONG 9: **Off To The Rescue**

They all sing except Fairy Lethargia, who joins in at an appropriate moment

Off through the forest
Off to the castle
Off to the rescue we race;
Summon up courage
Tackle the Monster
Challenge the Giant and put those two Wolves in their place;
We must find her
We can't be that far behind her
We'll follow the track
And bring our Goose back
Leave no stone unturned
Till we have returned
With her found
Safe and sound.

Off through the forest
Off to the castle
Off to the rescue we race;
Nothing can stop us
We won't be beaten
We'll do our best for our quest must be no wild goose chase:
When we see her
Somehow we'll force them to free her
We know that it's right
We'll stand up and fight
Then back to the Book
By hook or by crook
We'll vamoose
With our Goose!
Off to the rescue
Off the the rescue ...

Suddenly Little Jack Horner trips over something and falls over. He shouts out. The music stops, all except a tremolo rumble of excitement

Little Miss Muffet Enjoy your trip?

Little Jack Horner (*getting up*) There's something there—in that patch of grass.

They look. Suddenly Little Polly Flinders finds something

Little Polly Flinders Look.
Little Miss Muffet An egg.
Mother Goose A *golden* egg. It's beautiful.
Little Tommy Tucker Gertie must have laid it ...
Little Bo Peep So she *is* the Goose that laid the Golden Egg.
Fairy Lethargia (*taking control*) That's right. She was so grateful to you all for showing her kindness that she laid it for you.

(*Into couplets—but not sent up*)

> Throughout your quest, this egg will be your lucky charm
> As long as you don't lose it, you can come to no harm.

Little Bo Peep Thank you, Gertie.
Little Tommy Tucker We'll pay you back.

Little Polly Flinders ⎤
Little Miss Muffet ⎬ We're on our way! ⎰ (*speaking together*)
Little Jack Horner ⎦

SONG 9: **Off To The Rescue** (*continued*)

All   Off to the rescue
       Off to the rescue
       This Golden Egg will protect us from danger we know
       So
       Off to the rescue
       We go.

   As the song ends, the "quest" exits

Fairy Lethargia waves farewell. Then she replaces her wand on the Christmas tree, yawns and stretches and gets back into the decorations box. The music swells as the lighting narrows down to the star on the wand. Then it fades to a BLACK-OUT

The Christmas tree, with the wand on it as a star, remains in view throughout the Interval

ACT II

Scene 1

N.B. *This scene is optional. Its function is to re-establish the plot, but this may be felt to be unnecessary*

The Edge of the Forest (front cloth), with the Giant's Castle visible in the distance

The entr'acte music becomes sinister as the House Lights go down

The Wolves enter, dragging Gertie behind them. She still has the sack over her head. The Wolves savagely push and pull her, playing up to the audience reaction against them. Finally they exit the other side. The music changes, and from off we hear singing. The "Quest" then enters continuing the song. Little Polly Flinders still carries her kettle. Mother Goose has put on her dress and carries her dressing-gown

SONG 9A: **Off To The Rescue** (*reprise*)

Mother Goose, Little Miss Muffet, Little Jack Horner, Little Bo Peep, Little Tommy Tucker, Little Polly Flinders } (*singing together*)

Off through the forest
Off to the castle
Off to the rescue we race
Summon up courage
Tackle the Monster
Challenge the Giant and put those two Wolves in their place;
We must find her
We can't be that far behind her ...

The Music continues under the following dialogue

Little Miss Muffet (*excited*) There's the castle. It's not far.
Little Bo Peep Looks really spooky. (*Wanting reassurance*) Where's the golden egg?
Little Jack Horner Tommy's eaten it.
Little Tommy Tucker I haven't.
Mother Goose Here it is. (*She takes it from her pocket*)
Little Polly Flinders (*whispering in amazement*) It's bigger.
Mother Goose What, dear?
Little Polly Flinders The egg's grown. It's bigger.
Mother Goose So it is.
Little Jack Horner How eggstraordinary! Tara!

All groan at the pun

SONG 9A: Off To The Rescue (*reprise*) (*continued*)

All   Off to the rescue
            Off to the rescue
            Our Golden Egg will protect us from danger we know
            So
            Off to the rescue
            We go

As the song ends, they all exit towards the Castle

The Lights fade to a BLACK-OUT

SCENE 2

The Entrance to the Giant's Castle

Huge studded double doors dominate the scene upstage—giving an idea of the gigantic scale of the Castle. In front of the doors is a raised drawbridge. A sign says "BEWARE OF THE MONSTER OF THE MOAT", and downstage is a bank, to suggest the moat between it and the doors. Perhaps a lighting effect could suggest water reflections from the moat. On the bank side is a bell-push or bell-rope; if it is the latter, it could extend up into the flies, as though going up to a bell tower. Another sign says "RING THE BELL AND UTTER THE PASSWORD"

The Wolves enter dragging Gertie

Bigger Badder Wolf Ring the bell.
Big Bad Wolf What?
Bigger Badder Wolf Ring the bell.
Big Bad Wolf (*nervously*) I'd rather not.
Bigger Badder Wolf What do you mean (*imitating*) "I'd rather not"? We can't get inside unless we ring the bell.
Big Bad Wolf You ring it, then.
Bigger Badder Wolf Why me?
Big Bad Wolf You're more musical than I am.
Bigger Badder Wolf Don't be so stupid. What's the matter with you. Why won't you ring the bell?
Big Bad Wolf It m-m-means m-m-moving towards the m-m-moat and the M-m-m-monster.
Bigger Badder Wolf The Monster isn't worried about you.
Big Bad Wolf No, but I'm a little worried about *him*.
Bigger Badder Wolf Oh, for wickedness sake—hold this horrible bird.

The Big Bad Wolf does so. The Bigger Badder Wolf strides confidently up to the bell-rope and pulls it. He returns

There you are. Nothing to it.

The very loud boom of the deep, ominous, clanging bell, makes them both jump.

From high up in the flies we hear the sound of a sash window being raised. The Wolves look up

Giant's Voice (*booming down from the flies*) Password.
Bigger Badder Wolf Password.
Bigger Badder Wolf ⎫ Copper and silver leave us cold ⎰ (*chanting*
Big Bad Wolf ⎭ What we want is lots of gold. ⎱ *together*)
Giant's Voice Again.
Bigger Badder Wolf Why? Don't you believe us?
Giant's Voice Yes. But I enjoy hearing it.
Bigger Badder Wolf ⎫ Copper and silver leave us cold ⎰ (*chanting*
Big Bad Wolf ⎭ What we want is lots of gold. ⎱ *together*)
Giant's Voice You may enter.
Bigger Badder Wolf Thanks, Boss. We've got the Goose.
Giant's Voice Splendid. (*He laughs—a hollow, evil, booming laugh*)

With a sinister creaking sound, the drawbridge lowers, and clanks on to the bank. Music, as the Wolves and Gertie start to go across. The Big Bad Wolf is nervous, and surreptitiously takes out a tranquillizer and pops it in his mouth. The Bigger Badder Wolf catches him at it, and slaps him on the back. The gob-stopper-size tranquillizer pops out—into the moat. The Wolves react worried, and even more so when they hear the sound of the Monster, underwater, being woken up, hit by the flying gob-stopper—a sort of "ow" sound, followed by a roar of anger. The Wolves cling on to each other as well as Gertie, as, suddenly, an enormous head—rather like the head of the Loch Ness Monster—rears up from the moat, and advances towards them, snapping its jaws and uttering frightening sounds

The Wolves manage to edge their way along the drawbridge, pushing Gertie ahead of them. They reach the doors, enter the castle—more sinister creaking sounds—and close the doors

The drawbridge raises itself, perhaps hitting the Monster on the "chin" as it does so. The Monster, disappointed, returns under the water with a dissatisfied moan. The music continues

Little Miss Muffet enters downstage, and beckons on Mother Goose and the other Children. They enter on tiptoe. Mother Goose still carries her dressing-gown—she puts it down in a suitable place during the following scene

Little Jack Horner (*loudly*) Cor, it's gigantic!
All Shhhh!

They all huddle downstage, organized by Mother Goose, and start to whisper tactics. They are stopped by the booming sound of the Giant's voice

Giant's Voice (*from the flies above*) Hallo, Goosey, Goosey. Welcome home. Ha, ha, ha. Into your cage, there's a good bird.

There is the clank of a cage door closing and a key turning

Now, back on the job. I want a Golden Egg, do you hear? A Golden Egg. And if you don't lay it soon, you'll be shut in a dungeon without food or water till you rot. So lay, blast you, lay.

Giant footsteps are heard retreating. Mother Goose and the Children react to the speech, shaking their fists up towards the flies

Little Jack Horner (*loudly, incensed*) Mother Goose …
All Sssh.
Little Jack Horner (*whispering*) Mother Goose, let me rescue Gertie from that big bully Bossyboots. Let Little Jack Horner be Jack the Giant-killer.
Mother Goose It's your story, dear; so good luck.
All Good luck, Jack. Take care, etc.
Mother Goose Don't forget the Golden Egg. (*She hands it to him*)

                    *   *   *   *   *

The following three speeches should be inserted if Act II Scene I has been omitted

Little Polly Flinders The egg's grown. It's bigger.
Mother Goose So it is.
Little Jack Horner How eggstraordinary. Tara!

                    *   *   *   *   *

Little Bo Peep How are you going to get in the Castle?
Little Jack Horner I'll swim across the moat.
Little Tommy Tucker But look (*he points to the sign—"BEWARE OF THE MONSTER OF THE MOAT"*)—"Beware of the Monster of the Moat."
Little Jack Horner I'm not frightened of a Monster—I've got the Golden Egg.

Dramatic rumble music as Little Jack Horner approaches the moat. The others huddle together, watching. Little Jack Horner stands on the edge of the bank and flexes his legs and arms as if to dive into the moat. As an afterthought, he turns back and waves to the "family". As he does so, the Monster's head rears up, unseen by him, but visible to the others and to the audience. All try to warn him. He smiles disbelievingly, and turns back to find himself virtually nose to nose with the Monster. He screams and jumps impulsively, and in his panic to escape, throws his arms in the air, allowing the Golden Egg to fly from his hand and fall into the watery depths of the moat. A splash sound effect could enhance this. The Monster disappears again, the "threat" having gone

Little Miss Muffet Now look what you've done.
Little Jack Horner (*hardly able to believe it*) I'm sorry. I jumped.
Little Tommy Tucker So did the Golden Egg. Right into the moat.
Little Bo Peep (*on the verge of tears*) We'll never rescue Gertie now.
Little Miss Muffet What can we do? Mother Goose?
Mother Goose Is it an emergency?
Little Bo Peep (*emotionally*) Of course it is. We must get the Golden Egg back.
Mother Goose If it's an emergency, there's only one thing to do—

Pause, during which the audience may call out, "Get Fairy Lethargia"—

Little Polly Flinders (*eventually, whispering*) Call Lethargia.
Mother Goose What, dear?

Little Polly Flinders (*louder*) Call Fairy Lethargia.

Mother Goose Bullseye! Come on, everyone: (*Looking at the castle*) But not too loudly. One, two, three.

All
Audience } Fairy Lethargia. { (*calling together*)

They look towards the decorations box—still in position at the side of the stage

A loud yawn heralds Fairy Lethargia's arrival from the box

Fairy Lethargia Up, down, up, down, up, down. I'm not a flipping Jack-in-the-Box, you know.

Mother Goose It's an emergency.

Fairy Lethargia It always is. (*Suddenly noticing the castle*) Oo-er. Where are we? I'll say this much. Your story's very moving.

Little Tommy Tucker Moving?

Fairy Lethargia Yes—it's never in the same place twice. Just as well I don't get travel-sick. Whose is this humble abode, eh?

Little Miss Muffet The Giant's.

Fairy Lethargia Ooh, I don't like giants.

Little Miss Muffet Why not?

Fairy Lethargia They always look down on people! Right, come on. (*She yawns*) I can't hang around all afternoon. I thought this was an emergency.

Little Bo Peep (*crossly*) It is. But you won't let us get a word in edgeways.

Fairy Lethargia Ooooh! Hark at her. Fairies have feelings, you know. I know when I'm not wanted. (*She yawns*) Night, night. (*She starts to climb back into the box*)

Mother Goose You've offended her now. Fairy Lethargia, please you must help.

Fairy Lethargia Why? You're all right. You've got the Golden Egg. Night.

Little Jack Horner But that's the whole point. We haven't.

Fairy Lethargia Eh? (*She stops*)

Little Jack Horner (*sheepishly, pointing to the moat*) I dropped the egg in the water.

Fairy Lethargia (*after a pause to take in the news*) You dropped the egg in the water? Knowing you, I'm surprised you didn't add a pinch of salt, turn the gas on and boil it for three minutes. All right, I'll help. You'll have to dredge the bed of the moat. Like looking for buried treasure.

Little Miss Muffet We *are* looking for buried treasure.

Mother Goose What can we use to try and scoop it up?

The audience may shout out solutions

Little Polly Flinders (*eventually*) We could try my kettle! (*She holds it up*) And I've got some string ... (*She produces the string and starts to tie it on the handle*)

Little Tommy Tucker No, Polly, that'll never work. Anyway, I've made my mind up. *I'm* going to find it—like a pearl diver.

Mother Goose You're most certainly not, Tommy dear. Not with Daughter of Dracula in there gnashing her mashers.

Little Tommy Tucker If Jack can grapple with the giant, I can mix it with a Monster.

Fairy Lethargia Fighting words, Little Tommy T. But why not use Polly's kettle too?

Little Tommy Tucker How?

Fairy Lethargia Stand there and I'll show you! (*She positions him*) Right. A bit of hush, please. A bit of atmosphere.

SONG 9B: **Fairy Lethargia's Magic Spell** (*reprise*)

Fairy Lethargia   Spell number two is on Tommy
                             Him with the little fat tum ...

Little Tommy Tucker (*speaking*) Here! No need to be personal.

The Others Shhh.

Fairy Lethargia Don't be so touchy. The magic has to know who to work on ...

Little Tommy Tucker It's all very well ...

Fairy Lethargia Oh, all right, I'll start again.
                             (*She sings*) Spell Number Two is on Tommy
                             Another young Tom he'll become;
                             Abracadabra, hocus pocus
                             Magic him into Tom Thumb

As the spell ends, there is a flash and a bang, and magically Little Tommy Tucker disappears. Perhaps a trap could be used for this, in conjunction with a flash box, or a very short BLACK-OUT *would effect it. In his place there is a similarly dressed doll about nine inches high. The music continues*

Mother Goose Oo-er! Tommy! He's gone.

Fairy Lethargia No, he hasn't. Look.

Mother Goose sees the doll

Mother Goose Oh, Tommy, I know I kept saying you ought to diet, but I didn't mean it, dear, I didn't mean it!

Fairy Lethargia Shh. Polly, put Tom Thumb in your kettle.

Very gently, Polly does so

  Now, lower the kettle into the moat ...

Mother Goose Take care, dear. Tommy's in your hands.

Gingerly, Little Polly Flinders picks up the kettle, holding it by the string. Suddenly the Lighting snaps to BLACK-OUT, *all except for a follow spot on Little Polly Flinders. The action freezes as she sings*

SONG 9C: **My Big Moment** (*reprise*)

Little Polly Flinders   This must be my big moment
                             My moment of glory
                             In the story
                             This will be my closest shave
                             This must be my big moment
                             This is my time to be brave

Little Polly Flinders turns and makes her way towards the moat. The Lights fade to a BLACK-OUT, *and the scene changes very rapidly.* N.B. *It may be possible to start the scene change during the song 9C—perhaps by bringing in black tabs behind Little Polly Flinders*

SCENE 3

In the moat

MUSIC 10

The following sequence, which takes place underwater, is all mimed and moved to music. It could possibly be done in U.V. lighting, or using "black art", or it could be done using projection or lighting effects, depending on the scale of the production and the facilities available. It should take place downstage of the "entrance to the Giant's Castle" set, because the change back, as well as the change into the underwater sequence, should be very quick. The sequence is "magnified", so that "Tom Thumb" can be played by the normal-sized Tommy. Therefore, in due course, the kettle, the Monster and the Golden Egg should all be "blown up" versions. N.B. *The Monster cannot realistically be expected to be to scale. The overall effect of the sequence, apart from the exciting nature of Tommy's venture underwater, could be one of pure magic—using all the best "tricks" the theatre can offer*

The scene underwater could be enhanced by rocks and waving weeds. To start with there could be a "ballet" of fishes of different shapes and sizes. With a large cast, these could be actors, but the effect could be gained in U.V. lighting with cut-outs on rods operated by puppeteers dressed in black; or, perhaps projection or large "mobiles" operated from the flies could achieve it. Then the huge kettle arrives, as though let down by Little Polly Flinders on the string. Ideally it floats in gently from the flies and comes to rest on the bed of the moat, scattering the fishes. If this is impractical, the scene could start with the kettle already in position. The kettle will most probably be a cut-out—an enlargement of the normal-sized one

"Tom Thumb" clambers out of the kettle. The actor can enter between the tabs after the kettle has flown in, and climb over the cut-out. He looks warily about, then starts searching for the Golden Egg—behind rocks, weeds, etc. When he is out of sight, the Monster of the moat enters; played by four or more actors, each one a "segment". It is long like a centipede, all the legs moving in unison. It is not unlike the Loch Ness Monster, perhaps, but the head looks frightening, its jaws snapping as it stomps along. Clearly, from the audience point of view, it should look amusing as well as frightening. Suddenly, after a "dance" around, it sees the kettle and reacts startled—a jolt going from segment to segment, accompanied by the relevant feet jumping back in surprise

The Monster goes to examine the kettle more carefully. Perhaps the head peeps behind it, or perhaps the whole body investigates the back of it. At the same time "Tom Thumb" struggles back with the "blown-up" Golden Egg—about

*his own height. A cut-out is more practical than a shaped object. He starts strug-
gling to put the Golden Egg inside the kettle. With a great effort he manages
it, but just before it disappears from view the Monster re-emerges and sees it—
and "Tom Thumb". Stamping its feet in fury, it backs away ready to "charge".
Tom, still at ground level, sees the Monster, reacts with fear; then the action
freezes, the Lighting dramatically changes to a follow spot on "Tom Thumb"
and the music goes into "My Big Moment", which "Tom Thumb" mimes. It
could be amusing to have a garbled underwater singing voice off. Then the Lighting and the action revert to their former states*

*Now follows an exciting moved/choreographed section during which the monster
"charges" "Tom Thumb", who has to nip sharply out of the way. Perhaps he
could acrobatically "leapfrog", in stages from segment to segment. At least twice
he manages to escape the "charge". Then the Monster adopts a subtler approach
and attempts to "surround" "Tom Thumb" with itself—the head and the tail
meeting. He escapes between the feet. Then, surrounding him again, the Monster
does his "coup"—it divides into individual segments, as many as the actors inside,
each of which has its own face, and, ideally, snapping jaws. This can be incorporated effectively into a visually exciting pattern, as "Tom Thumb" weaves
his way in and out of the little Monsters.*

*Finally he tricks them, perhaps by encouraging them to advance on him like a
rugby scrum, then escaping, leaving them heads together in a circle, revolving.
He climbs back up into the kettle, not forgetting to give two big tugs on the
string. He disappears inside*

*The kettle rises up, as if pulled by Little Polly Flinders. The Monster or
Monsters, frustrated, watch it go. The Lights fade to a* BLACK-OUT

SCENE 4

The Entrance to the Giant's Castle

*The scene changes back, as speedily as possible, to the position at the end of
Scene 2. Little Polly Flinders is pulling the kettle up from the bed of the moat,
watched by the other Children and Mother Goose, with Fairy Lethargia, who
has nodded off again. Little Polly Flinders carefully brings the kettle downstage.
The others cluster round.*

Little Bo Peep Well?
Little Polly Flinders (*producing the egg*) He's done it! Look.
Little Miss Muffet (*gasping*) It's grown again. It's twice the size!

Indeed it has grown

Little Jack Horner How eggsciting! Tara!

All groan

Mother Goose Children, less levity, more gravity. Where's our Little Tommy?
Little Polly Flinders (*taking out the doll*) Here he is.

(*Speaking*) Of course, you don't *have* to whistle a tune. Any ideas?

Little Miss Muffet comes forward

Little Miss Muffet
When you're feeling worried
And your skies are looking grey
Try physical jerks
It always works.

Little Miss Muffet
Mother Goose }
Just whistle a tune
(*Whistle*)
And very soon
Your worry will hurry away.

Little Tommy Tucker
When you're feeling worried
And your skies are looking grey
Eat treacly pud
And you'll feel good.

Little Tommy Tucker
Little Miss Muffet
Mother Goose }
Try physical jerks
It always works
Just whistle a tune
(*Whistle*)
And very soon
Your worry will hurry away.

Little Bo Peep
When you're feeling worried
And your skies are looking grey
Try bouncing a ball
Against a wall.

Little Bo Peep
Little Tommy Tucker
Little Miss Muffet
Mother Goose }
Eat treacly pud
And you'll feel good
Try physical jerks
It always works
Just whistle a tune
(*Whistle*)
And very soon
Your worry will hurry away.

Little Polly Flinders
When you're feeling worried
And your skies are looking grey
Go pick up a broom
And sweep the room.

Little Polly Flinders
Little Bo Peep
Little Tommy Tucker
Little Miss Muffet
Mother Goose }
Try bouncing a ball
Against a wall
Eat treacly pud
And you'll feel good
Try physical jerks
It always works
Just whistle a tune

(*Whistle*)
And very soon
Your worry will hurry away.

During the last chorus, Fairy Lethargia is woken up by the noise, and pops out of the decorations box to see what is going on. She decides to join in

Fairy Lethargia   When you're feeling worried
                                     And your skies are looking grey
                                     Just have a good yawn
                                     And sleep till dawn

Fairy Lethargia   ⎫   Go pick up a broom
Little Polly Flinders   ⎪   And sweep the room
Little Bo Peep   ⎬   Try bouncing a ball
Little Tommy Tucker   ⎪   Against a wall
Little Miss Muffet   ⎪   Eat treacly pud
Mother Goose   ⎭   And you'll feel good
                                     Try physical jerks
                                     It always works
                                     Just whistle a tune
                                     (*Whistle*)
                                     And very soon
                                     Your worry will hurry away.

All   When you're feeling worried
                                     And your skies are looking grey
                                     Start marching along
                                     And sing this song
                                     Just have a good yawn
                                     And sleep till dawn
                                     Go pick up a broom
                                     And sweep the room
                                     Try bouncing a ball
                                     Against a wall
                                     Eat treacly pud
                                     And you'll feel good
                                     Try physical jerks
                                     It always works
                                     Just whistle a tune
                                     (*Whistle*)
                                     And very soon
                                     Your worry will hurry
                                     Your worry will hurry
                                     Your worry will hurry away.
          (*Shouting*)   Don't worry!

At the end of the song, all the Children have cheered up

Mother Goose There you are. Are you still worried about Jack?

Children No.
Mother Goose Good. Mother Goose was right, wasn't she?
Children Yes.

Mother Goose suddenly frowns and bites her nails and taps her foot nervously and scratches her neck, etc. Then she starts whistling

Little Polly Flinders What's the matter, Mother Goose?
Mother Goose Oooh. I'm so worried I can't stand it. (*She calls*) Jack. Jack. I'm coming to help you, dear.

   Mother Goose grabs her dressing-gown and runs off

   (*As she goes*) Go home, children. And don't worry!

Ideally Mother Goose would dash along the drawbridge into the castle, just before it closes: but perhaps she runs off and as the Lights fade to a BLACK-OUT *we hear the clanking sound of the drawbridge rising, thus giving the impression that she has just made it in time*

SCENE 5

The Giant's Workshop

In this set, everything is magnified. There is a high window, open, and an over-grown chair and table, which stretches off, thus making the table-top accessible from the wings one side. The chair should be constructed in such a way that normal-sized people can use it as a stepping-stone to the table-top. On the table is a cage with a barred door; Gertie is inside. Throughout the whole set there should be not a trace of the colour gold. On stage level are several steaming cauldrons, foaming beakers, test tubes, etc., and tomes piled high. To one side is a giant oven, with a dial marked "OFF", "ON", "HOT", "HOTTER", and "OUCH". On a shelf or side table are visible several large tins or jars, marked "CUSTARD POWDER", "MUSTARD POWDER", "GUN POWDER", "CHOWDER POWDER", "ITCHING POWDER", "TALCUM POWDER". A vase of daffodils and a lighted candle are also visible. The large tomes are open, covers facing the audience: "TEACH YOURSELF ALCHEMY" and "GOLD-MAKING FOR BEGINNERS"

As the scene starts, the heads of the two Wolves menacingly creep up over the books. They laugh nastily. The heads return to their reading. Suddenly Bigger Badder Wolf speaks

Bigger Badder Wolf Aha! Here's an experiment we haven't tried.
Big Bad Wolf Aha! (*He tries to imitate the Bigger Badder Wolf, but it turns into a cough*) Read it out, B.B.W.
Bigger Badder Wolf (*reading slowly and deliberately*) How to make a bar of gold. (*He rubs his hands in anticipation*)
Big Bad Wolf A bar of gold!
Bigger Badder Wolf Take one heavy brick.
Big Bad Wolf One heavy brick. (*He finds one, and staggers with the weight*)

Bigger Badder Wolf Drop it ...

Big Bad Wolf Drop it. (*He drops it on the Bigger Badder Wolf's foot*)

Bigger Badder Wolf Aaaaah! What did you do that for?

Big Bad Wolf You said "drop it".

Bigger Badder Wolf I hadn't finished. Drop it in a cauldron.

Big Bad Wolf Ah. Drop it in a cauldron. (*He does so*)

Bigger Badder Wolf Add one yellow daffodil.

Big Bad Wolf One yellow daffodil. (*He finds one, sniffs it, sneezes, and throws it in the cauldron*)

Bigger Badder Wolf (*lyrically*) Add the golden tones of the song of the yellow-hammer.

Big Bad Wolf Eh?

Bigger Badder Wolf The yellow-hammer.

Big Bad Wolf Oh. (*He produces a large yellow hammer—the sort for banging in nails*) Got one.

Bigger Badder Wolf (*not seeing, too busy reading the experiment*) Good. Make it sing.

The Big Bad Wolf looks mystified, then looks at the hammer and encouragingly "la las" a few notes. No reaction from the hammer

Big Bad Wolf B.B.W.

Bigger Badder Wolf Mm?

Big Bad Wolf The yellow hammer doesn't want to sing.

Bigger Badder Wolf Well, bash it on the head.

Big Bad Wolf Eh?

Bigger Badder Wolf (*impatiently*) Bash it on the head.

After a doubting pause, the Big Bad Wolf smashes the hammer down on the Bigger Badder Wolf's head

OW! What are you doing? What's this?

Big Bad Wolf A yellow hammer.

Bigger Badder Wolf For wickedness sake! I meant a bird, a yellow-hammer bird. Oh, never mind. Stir in a spoonful of custard powder.

The Big Bad Wolf runs his hand along the jars or tins, calling them out as he goes

Big Bad Wolf Talcum powder, itching powder, chowder powder, gun powder, mustard powder, custard powder.

He takes down the jar and pours some in. He replaces the jar

Bigger Badder Wolf (*before the Big Bad Wolf has finished, making him hurry*) And a pinch of mustard powder.

The Big Bad Wolf dashes back, and, by mistake, takes down the gun powder. He pours some in. The audience must realize his mistake

Big Bad Wolf Mustard powder. One pinch of. (*He replaces the jar*)

Bigger Badder Wolf Expose to the golden rays of the sun.

Big Bad Wolf We can't. There's no sun today. (*Pointing out of the window*) It's cloudy.

Bigger Badder Wolf We'll have to find a substitute. (*He looks around*) Ah. Try the golden rays of that candle instead.
Big Bad Wolf Oh, right.
He takes the lighted candle and throws it in the cauldron. Immediately there is a loud explosion and smoke from the cauldron. The impact knocks the Wolves over. As they recover, the Bigger Badder Wolf starts hitting the Big Bad Wolf. Suddenly the Giant's voice is heard

Giant's Voice (*Off*) Wolves! Wolves!

They spring to attention

Bigger Badder Wolf Yes, Boss?
Big Bad Wolf Y-y-yes, B-b-boss?
Giant's Voice Any Golden Eggs from that Goose yet?
Bigger Badder Wolf Just checking, Boss. (*He deliberately takes the large key to the cage from inside his coat and hands it to the Big Bad Wolf*) Cage. (*He glances to the cage on the table above*)
Big Bad Wolf (*realising the implication*) Oh n-no, n-no, n-not m-me, p-please.
Bigger Badder Wolf Why not you?
Big Bad Wolf You know I can't stand heights. I'll get giddy. I'll have one of my turns. (*He reaches for a tranquillizer*)
Bigger Badder Wolf Oh, come on then.
Music, as he pushes the Big Bad Wolf to the chair

A brief comic interlude as they climb up—the Big Bad Wolf falling on or stepping on the Bigger Badder Wolf, who pushes him on ahead.

Eventually they reach the cage, unlock the door and, pushing Gertie aside, look inside. They shake their heads and close and lock the door. The music stops

Nothing. We'd better go and tell him.
Big Bad Wolf (*nervously*) Ooh.

The music starts again as the Wolves exit along the table into the wings— towards where the Giant is presumably sitting at the other end

After a pause, Little Jack Horner enters from the opposite side. He takes in the huge furniture and creeps about checking nobody is around. He puts his finger to his mouth to make sure the audience remain quiet and don't give the game away

Little Jack Horner spots Gertie in the cage; or it may be better for him to whisper "Where's Gertie?" to the audience, and incorporate their help—not vocally, but pointing to the cage. He climbs up the chair and arrives on the table. He tiptoes to the cage

Little Jack Horner (*whispering*) Gertie! Psst. It's me, Jack.

Gertie rushes excitedly to the bars, flapping her wings

Shhhh. I've come to rescue you. (*He tries the cage door*) Where's the key?
Gertie indicates the Wolves off, and the audience, not forgetting to whisper, interpret

The Wolves. Oh. (*He ponders what to do*)

Mother Goose, still carrying her dressing-gown, enters stealthily

Mother Goose (*whispering*) Jack, Jack.

Jack jumps in surprise, then recovers and looks down from the table top, just as Mother Goose is passing below, so her back is now turned away from him

Little Jack Horner (*in a loud whisper*) Mother Goose!

Mother Goose nearly has a heart attack and ducks under the chair seat. Jack slips from the table on to the chair seat. He kneels, then slowly slides his head over the edge; simultaneously Mother Goose slowly slides her head out from underneath. The heads meet, making Mother Goose and Little Jack Horner nearly jump out of their skins

Mother Goose (*recovering*) Oh, it's you, dear. What a relief. I'm all of a quiver. Like a nervous jelly.

Little Jack Horner (*whispering*) Shhh!

The sudden roar of the Giant's voice is heard, off

Giant's Voice What? Still no Golden Egg? Right, Goosey Goosey; you've had your last chance. Ha, ha, ha, ha.

The laughter approaches

Little Jack Horner (*whispering*) Quick, he's coming. Gertie's locked in the cage up here but the Wolves have the key.

Mother Goose (*after a pause, whispering*) I know, dear. Put the Golden Egg in the cage. The Giant will want it, the Wolves will have to open the cage to take it out, and ... (*she is too late*)

Giant's Voice (*calling*) Goosey Goosey! Ha, ha, ha, ha.

Mother Goose retreats under the chair. Jack leaps back on to the table and carefully puts the Golden Egg through the bars of the cage. Then he spots a dining fork—large scale—on the table top, and arms himself with it. Finally he hides at the side of the cage

> *Suddenly, the Wolves enter, on the table, leading in the Giant, who should naturally be as large as possible. It may be an idea to use another actor's voice from a microphone off, so that a huge headmask could be employed*

SONG 12: **Fee Fi Fo Fum**

During the song, the Wolves climb down from the table via the chair. Mother Goose, hiding, looks terrified as the Wolves pass so near her

Giant	Fee fi fo fum
	I am the Giant, here I come
	Fee fi fo fum
	Goosey for dinner, yum yum yum.
	Fee
Wolves	Fee
Giant	Fi

Wolves	Fi
Giant	Fo
Wolves	Fo
Giant	Fum
Wolves	Fum
Giant	I am the Giant, here I come.
	Fee
Wolves	Fee
Giant	Fi
Wolves	Fi
Giant	Fo
Wolves	Fo
Giant	Fum
Wolves	Fum
Giant	Goosey, Prepare to meet my tum.

Giant (*speaking*) Wolves!
Wolves Yes, Boss?
Giant Light the oven.
Wolves Yes, Boss.

The Wolves go to the oven and turn the dial, which makes an unpleasant ratchet noise, gleefully through "HOT", and "HOTTER" to "OUCH". Gertie is reacting

Giant We'll see if Goosey Goosey tastes better than she works. Ha, ha, ha, ha.

The Bigger Badder Wolf opens the oven door a little—a red glow tells us the oven is on

Stubborn bird. All I wanted was one Golden Egg.

The audience may well shout out, "look in the cage"

(*Eventually*) But you wouldn't lay. So now you'll pay. Wolves!
Wolves Yes, Boss?
Giant Open the cage.
Wolves Yes, Boss.

The Bigger Badder Wolf deliberately hands the key to the Big Bad Wolf

Big Bad Wolf Oh, no, please, not again ...
Bigger Badder Wolf Go on. Hurry up.
Giant (*roaring*) What are you muttering about?
Bigger Badder Wolf Nothing, Boss.
Big Bad Wolf N-n-nothing, B-b-boss.

Reluctantly the Big Bad Wolf climbs up on to the table. A dramatic drum roll as he approaches the cage. He puts the key in the lock, turns it and opens the door

Come on, Goosey Goosey.

Leaving the key in the lock, he grabs Gertie, who tries to point out the Golden Egg. This proves difficult, and she is pulled out of the cage and a few steps away from it before the Big Bad Wolf realizes

It's no use struggling, I'm too strong ... (*If the audience are shouting*) What? (*He suddenly spots the Golden Egg*) Hey! She's done it! She's done it! B-boss, l-look—a Golden Egg. (*He takes it reverently from the cage—it is quite large now, say eighteen inches high—and holds it out*)

Giant (*roaring*)   What? Aaaaaaah! At last, at last! Gold. Real gold. Ah ha ha ha.

The Giant takes the Golden Egg and, roaring with laughter, does the nearest a Giant can to hopping about with joy, stroking and kissing the Golden Egg.

The Big Bad Wolf stands smiling on the table top. The Bigger Badder Wolf is still by the oven.

Music. Little Jack Horner creeps round from his hiding place by the cage and prods the Big Bad Wolf with the outsize fork. The Big Bad Wolf nearly has heart failure—he could have fallen over the edge! He turns, sees Little Jack Horner and reacts terrified. Little Jack Horner stalks him round with the fork. Meanwhile Gertie hangs back by the cage door and the Bigger Badder Wolf is too busy watching the ecstatic Giant to notice. Suddenly the Big Bad Wolf has an idea. He brings out his tranquillizers and starts throwing them at Little Jack Horner, who has to use the fork as a shield: but the tranquillizers run out, and the Big Bad Wolf puts up his hands in submission. Little Jack Horner forces him at fork point back, round and into the cage, the door of which Gertie holds open for him. They slam the door shut, turn the key and remove it from the lock. They raise their arms/wings in triumph

Mother Goose manages to peep out occasionally from under the chair, and glean some idea of Little Jack Horner's progress. Now, she watches him bring the key of the cage to the edge of the table top. He indicates he is going to throw it down and she stands by to catch it.

He throws, but she misses, and it hits the floor. The sound is heard by the Bigger Badder Wolf, who turns and sees Mother Goose. In a rage, he advances on her. She picks up the key and tries to fend him off with it. He grabs the other end and they have a heave-ho tug-of-war with it, ending with the Bigger Badder Wolf tripping over a tome and falling: But Mother Goose has let go of the end of the key, and soon the Bigger Badder Wolf is up again, advancing on her, using the key as a weapon.

Mother Goose looks wildly around and spots her dressing-gown, which is a red one. There follows a short, amusing bullfighting sequence to appropriate music, with Mother Goose using her dressing-gown as a cape, and the Bigger Badder Wolf charging her. On one of his charges, he overruns, bumping into the still drooling Giant, who notices, and turns—just in time to see the Bigger Badder Wolf charge in the other direction, towards Mother Goose, who has manœuvred herself to the oven. At the last minute she opens the door and the Bigger Badder Wolf charges straight into the red glowing oven. Mother Goose shuts the door, and raises her arms in a bullfighter's triumph. Little Jack Horner and Gertie have watched from above: But now the Giant is ranting and roaring and advancing towards the table, arms flailing with rage, that his henchmen have been disposed of. In his excitement he drops the Golden Egg, which is caught by Mother Goose below. Just as the Giant appears to aim a blow towards Little Jack Horner and Gertie, the action freezes and the Lighting changes to just a follow spot on Little Jack Horner

SONG 12A: **My Big Moment** (*reprise*)

Little Jack Horner   This must be my big moment
                             My moment of glory
                             In the story
                             This will be my closest shave,
                             This must be my big moment
                             This is my time to be brave.

The Lighting returns to its former state and the action resumes. Little Jack Horner and the Giant fight their duel—the action climax of the drama! The actual mechanical details of the combat will have to be left to the ingenuity of the individual directors, having regard for the capabilities and limitations of their Giant. Clearly a lavish production might have a Giant capable of more mobility and tricks—like picking up Little Jack Horner with one hand—than a more modest production: or some directors may feel it better to see the Giant only in silhouette, thus using back-projection on to a screen. Another idea is that the Giant could be a huge puppet, even operated from inside. It might be possible for Little Jack Horner to leap on the Giant's shoulders, or to have a sort of sword fight with him; the Giant could use his dagger and Little Jack Horner the fork. If the actor playing Little Jack Horner were athletic or acrobatic, further exciting ideas could develop, using ropes on which to swing to the ground, etc. Certainly Gertie should help the cause with the odd peck—her come-uppance against her cruel master adds an important element of poetic justice: and Mother Goose can shout encouragement; but she should not be actively involved in the battle, because this is Little Jack Horner's moment of glory. Naturally the contest ends in triumph for Little Jack Horner, as the Giant topples from the high window and falls to the moat below. A huge splash is followed by the snapping of jaws and the contented munching of the Monster of the moat. Victory yells of triumph from all, as Little Jack Horner climbs down the chair to floor-level, where Mother Goose hugs him

Little Jack Horner Back to the Book.
Mother Goose Take the Golden Egg, dear. It's grown again.
Little Jack Horner What we've come to eggspect! Tara!

Mother Goose groans. They set off for the exit. Meanwhile Gertie, on the table top, tries gingerly to put one foot down towards the chair in an attempt to get down. Now she flaps her wings. The audience may call out to Mother Goose and Little Jack Horner

   (*Eventually, suddenly remembering*) Gertie!
They turn back

(*Seeing Gertie*) Come on.

Gertie shakes her head and mimes flight

She can't get down, Mother Goose.

Mother Goose Cooped up in that cage for so long she can't fly any more.

Little Jack Horner But we can't leave without her. She's the reason we came.

Mother Goose Crisis time. (*To the audience, indicating the decorations box*) One, two, three.

All
Audience } Fairy Lethargia. { (*calling together*)

Pause

Fairy Lethargia (*in the box*) Co—ming!

> *Fairy Lethargia struggles, yawning, out of the decorations box and goes to collect her wand*
>
> Right. Spell Three. And you'd better look sharp. I'm so drained, my wings are beginning to droop and my wand's wilting. (*Turning and seeing the Giant's workshop*) Oo-er, I'm shrinking too!

Mother Goose No, you're not. We're in the Giant's workshop.

Fairy Lethargia Oh. Well, I don't like it. I want to go home.

Mother Goose So do we. But Gertie's stuck.

Gertie flaps her wings

Fairy Lethargia Right. No problem. You two—up on the table.

Little Jack Horner and Mother Goose climb up

> Huddle together and hang on tight. Fasten your seat belts for Spell Three. (*She comes forward*)

SONG 12B: **Fairy Lethargia's Magic Spell** (*reprise*)

It may be practical to bring in tabs behind Fairy Lethargia as she sings the spell, to facilitate the scene change, or the tabs could fly in behind the table, but in front of the rest of the Giant's workshop. This would mean that Gertie, Mother Goose and Little Jack Horner could be visible during the spell

Fairy Lethargia   Gertie and Jack and his Mother
All want to go home—so do I
Abracadabra, hocus pocus
Make us all able to fly.

At the end of the song, there is a flash, leading, as quickly as possible, into the following scene

SCENE 6

In the sky

MUSIC 13

We see Gertie in flight, complete with Mother Goose and Little Jack Horner "on board" her. They are joined by Fairy Lethargia flying under her own steam. This sequence should take only a minute or two, and can be done in several different ways:

(1) The table could become a platform on which they all stand, and lighting makes it look as though they are suspended in mid-air, flying
(2) Projection of moving clouds against the sky could give an impression of movement, plus, perhaps, some sort of wind machine off stage
(3) The whole thing could be done in U.V. lighting in front of black tabs. The sequence could start with small cut-out figures in rods, "walked across" by stage-hands clad in black, changing over to medium-sized ones, then ending up with the real characters, being pulled across on a black truck, invisible against the black tabs. Fairy Lethargia could be on a separate one
(4) Kirby's Flying Ballet

The scene could be very effective because it represents the traditional picture of Mother Goose of Nursery Rhyme fame—flying on a goose. Also, if it can be made to look magical, it will be a very exciting visual moment

Mother Goose You're flying, Gertie. This is your big moment
SONG: **Her Big Moment**

Mother Goose ⎫
Little Jack Horner ⎬   This must be her big moment
Fairy Lethargia ⎭   Her moment of glory
                     In the story
                     This must be her closest shave
                     This must be her big moment
                     This is her time to be brave
                     This must be her big moment
                     This is her time to be brave.

As the song ends, the Lights fade to a BLACK-OUT

SCENE 7

Back at the Book

As quickly as possible, the Lights go up on the "cover" side of the Book. It is dusk; Little Miss Muffet, Little Polly Flinders, Little Bo Peep and Little Tommy Tucker are putting the final touches to the Christmas decorations: but they are not happy—because they are worried about Mother Goose, Little Jack Horner and Gertie. A table of food lies untouched. During the song even Little Tommy Tucker refuses to eat anything

SONG 13A: **Getting Ready For Christmas** (*reprise*)

A slow, sad version

Little Miss Muffet ⎫	We're getting ready for Christmas
Little Bo Peep ⎪	We're getting ready for Christmas Day
Little Tommy Tucker ⎬	Building a snowman
Little Polly Flinders ⎭	From cotton-wool snow
	Hanging up the holly
	And the mistletoe ...

Suddenly they hear the loud beating of wings overhead. Dramatic musical rumble. They look up into the flies and follow Gertie's "progress" across the stage above their heads

Little Miss Muffet It's them! Look!

The others cheer, and "watch" Gertie land, off

SONG 13A: (*continued*)

The song speeds up

Little Miss Muffet ⎫	We're getting ready
Little Bo Peep ⎪	Getting ready for Christmas
Little Tommy Tucker ⎬	Ready
Little Polly Flinders ⎭	Steady—
	Go, go, go—

Mother Goose enters, with Jack Horner and Gertie. The others warmly greet them

All, with ⎫	
Mother Goose ⎬	Christmas
Little Jack Horner ⎭	Hallo.

At the end of the song, all chatter animatedly—"What happened?", "Did you see the Giant?", "Thank goodness you're safe", etc. etc.

Fairy Lethargia enters, almost on her knees with tiredness. She stands, looking at the excited "family group", none of whom see her

She coughs to get their attention. No reaction: and again: no reaction. So she puts her fingers in her mouth and does a vibrant, shrill whistle. All shut up and turn to her

Fairy Lethargia Is that it, then? Till next year? (*She yawns*) I can't twinkle much longer.

Mother Goose But Christmas Day hasn't begun yet!

Fairy Lethargia No, but the story's finished, isn't it? Must be; you've had your three spells.

Mother Goose Yes, almost. The Children wanted adventure, something out of the ordinary, and we've certainly had that; and they've all been so brave that I for one will never think of them as "Little" again. But, Fairy

Lethargia, you must keep your eyes open a little longer. It's time for our Christmas party. (*She calls*) POLLY!

Little Polly Flinders (*confidently*) Yes, Mother Goose?

Mother Goose Put the kettle on!

Laughter

Little Polly Flinders goes inside

Music, as Gertie comes forward and gently pecks Mother Goose, who turns. Gertie embraces her

Little Jack Horner She's saying thank you!

Gertie bows to all the Children

Mother Goose Well, Gertie, the best way you can thank us is to stay with us as long as you like. Right, everyone?

All nod and agree

Gertie suddenly runs off, nudging Little Jack Horner and Little Tommy Tucker off too

What's she up to now?

Gertie returns with the two boys carrying the Golden Egg—even larger, say thirty inches high—wrapped with ribbon and with a label. Gertie presents it to Mother Goose

For me? Oh, thank you, Gertie. It won't grow any more, will it?

Little Jack Horner It's getting a little eggcessive! Tara!

All groan

Mother Goose Oh, look, a label. (*Reading*)

Happy Christmas to you,
Happy Christmas to you,
Happy Christmas, dear Mother Goose,
Happy Christmas to you.

Thank you.

Gertie mimes singing

Little Jack Horner She says, let's sing it. Come on, then. Everybody.

SONG 14: **Happy Christmas To You**

The audience is encouraged to join in this, the equivalent of a songsheet

All, including audience ⎫
except Mother Goose ⎬ Happy Christmas to you
             ⎭ Happy Christmas to you
Happy Christmas dear Mother Goose
Happy Christmas to you.

Little Jack Horner (*speaking*) Once more. With eggstra voice!

All, including audience ⎫   Happy Christmas to you
except Mother Goose ⎭   Happy Christmas to you
                                Happy Christmas dear Mother Goose
                                Happy Christmas to you.

At the end of the song, the music continues as the Golden Egg, to everyone's surprise, starts moving. Then it "grows" arms and legs and a head. It in fact "hatches"

Mother Goose Hallo, dear. Who are you?
Humpty Dumpty Humpty Dumpty.
Mother Goose Humpty Dumpty?

SONG 15: **Humpty Dumpty Sat On A Wall**

Humpty Dumpty acts out his nursery rhyme

Humpty Dumpty   Humpty Dumpty sat on a wall
                           Humpty Dumpty had a great fall
                           All the king's horses and all the king's men
                           Couldn't put Humpty Dumpty together again.

At the end of the song, all clap

Mother Goose Thank you, Humpty Dumpty. You're a very welcome addition to my Nursery Rhyme family. And we'll all take care to see you don't fall off that wall too often.

Little Polly Flinders enters with the kettle

Little Polly Flinders Kettle's boiled!
Mother Goose Then it's time for the party.

Music, as Fairy Lethargia comes forward in her best rhyming couplet fashion

Fairy Lethargia   Now Mother Goose's story has been well and truly told'n
                          For her and for her family, this Christmas will be golden.

If possible, Fairy Lethargia waves her wand two or three times causing magical lighting changes to occur in stages, each accompanied by a musical chord

SONG 16: **Mother Goose's Golden Christmas**

During the song, if possible, the whole set, and perhaps some of the costumes, become enriched with gold—streamers, glitter, lights, etc. There is no reason why, as a gesture of goodwill, the "Baddies" should not arrive during the song, to be made welcome by Mother Goose and her Family. Thus the number could be a Curtain Call in itself—also, being the final number, the more singing voices on stage the merrier

All   It's Mother Goose's Golden Christmas
         So come and join in ev'ryone.

         So
         Come and join us
         Come and join us

Come on in
The party has begun
It's Mother Goose's Golden Christmas
Come and join us ev'ryone
It's Mother Goose's Golden Christmas
Come and join us ev'ryone.

It's a day we shall remember
Throughout the coming year
That golden day in December
When our troubles seem to disappear

So
Come and join us
Come and join us
Come on in
The party has begun
It's Mother Goose's Golden Christmas
Come and join us ev'ryone
It's Mother Goose's Golden Christmas
Come and join us ev'ryone.

Never mind the wintry weather
Forget the rain and snow
With all the fam'ly together
Celebrating in the fireside glow

So
Come and join us
Come and join us
Come on in
The party has begun
It's Mother Goose's Golden Christmas
Come and join us ev'ryone
It's Mother Goose's Golden Christmas
Come and join us ev'ryone.

So
Come and join us
Come and join us
Come on in
The party has begun
It's Mother Goose's Golden Christmas
Come and join us ev'ryone
It's Mother Goose's Golden Christmas
Come and join us ev'ryone.

Girls   So
          Come and join us
Boys   Come and join us

Girls   So
            Come and join us
Boys   So
            Come and join with Mother
Girls   It's Mother
All   Goose's Golden Christmas
            Come and join us ev'ryone.

Optional extra scene

At the end of the song, the cast bow, and the audience should think it is the end: but suddenly Little Bo Peep bursts into tears

Mother Goose Oh no, Bo Peep. What's the matter? We're all meant to be happy. It's the end of the story.

Little Bo Peep How can I be happy? I still haven't found my sheep. (*She sobs*)

Mother Goose Oh dear. We can't finish like this. Fairy Lethargia, can't you help?

Fairy Lethargia Well, I'm so tired, my magic's almost run out, but (*taking in the audience*) if everyone could chip in and give me a hand, I dare say ...

Mother Goose Oh, we will. (*To the audience*) Won't we?

All Yes.

Fairy Lethargia Right, then. After me.
      Abracadabra, help Bo Peep.

All Abracadabra, help Bo Peep.

Fairy Lethargia Hocus pocus, find her sheep.

All Hocus pocus, find her sheep.

Fairy Lethargia Smashing. Now, let's put it together and say it as loud as we can. After three. One, two, three.

All (*As Fairy Lethargia waves her magic wand*)
      Abracadabra, help Bo Peep
      Hocus pocus, find her sheep.

A flash; and then by magic, Little Bo Peep's sheep—real—are revealed. Perhaps they could "enter" from the decorations box or simply be led on stage. All cheer. Little Bo Peep is happy again

SONG 16: (*continued*)
            So
            Come and join us
            Come and join us
            Come on in
            The party has begun
            It's Mother Goose's Golden Christmas
            Come and join us ev'ryone
            It's Mother Goose's Golden Christmas
            Come and join us ev'ryone.

Girls   So
            Come and join us

Boys	Come and join us
Girls	So
	Come and join us
Boys	So
	Come and join with Mother
Girls	It's Mother
All	Goose's Golden Christmas
	Come and join us ev'ryone.

CURTAIN

FURNITURE AND PROPERTY LIST

ACT I

On stage: Scene 1: *The Book*

Large "Book" representing **Mother Goose's** house. *On it:* bell-rope with bell

Large dining-table. *On it:* crockery, cutlery, cereal in packet. *Under it:* basket

6 chairs

Cupboard. *In it:* various provisions, including packet of cereal

Hearth with cinders, hob, kettle, 6 mugs of tea

Oven

Scene 2: *The Forest*

Cut-out trees and borders

Holly bushes

Tuffet

Spider's lair

Scene 3: *The Book*

Overall and chef's cap set for **Mother Goose**

On table: bowls, trays, rolling-pin, spoons, dish of currants, baking tin, dusting powder, wooden spoon with pin attached, frying pan

At back of set: tray of specially prepared "dough"

Concealed near table: trick baking tin with "balloon" pudding

Scene 4: *The Forest*

As before, but strike **Spider's** lair

Small Golden Egg hidden in grass patch

Off stage: Broom (**Polly**)

Piece of pie (**Tommy Tucker**)

Crook (**Bo Peep**)

Christmas tree (**Children**)

Large box of decorations (**Children**)

Wand (**Fairy Lethargia**)

Bottle of pills (**Big Bad Wolf**)

Bowl of curds and whey with spoon, to go in basket (**Miss Muffet**)

Sheet of notepaper, pencil (**Big Bad Wolf**)

Sack (**Wolves**)

Personal: **Big Bad Wolf:** pocket-watch

ACT II

On stage: Scene 1: *Edge of the Forest* (optional)

Nil

Scene 2: *Giant's Castle entrance*

Huge studded doors
Drawbridge with Notice
Bell-rope with Notice

Scene 3: *Moat*

Waving weeds, rocks
Oversize kettle (cut-out)
Oversize Golden Egg (cut-out)

Scene 4: *Giant's Castle entrance*

As before

Scene 5: *Giant's Workshop*

(All items are oversize)
Chair
Table. *On it:* dining fork
Cage with barred door. *In it:* larger still Golden Egg
Steaming cauldrons, foaming beakers, test tubes, tomes
Huge oven with dial
Shelf with tins or jars of various powders
Vase of daffodils
Lighted candle
Yellow hammer

Scene 6: *In the Sky*

Nil

Scene 7: *The Book*

On table: various plates of food
Around tree: assorted decorations

Off stage: Larger still Golden Egg (**Mother Goose**)
Length of string (**Polly Flinders**)
Tom Thumb Doll (**Tommy Tucker**)
Still larger Golden Egg (in kettle) (**Polly Flinders**)
Large key (**Bigger Badder Wolf**)
Largest Golden Egg of all, with Humpty Dumpty (**Gertie**)
Ribbon and label on Egg
Streamers, glitter, etc. (**Stage Management**)
"Real" sheep (optional) (**Stage Management**)

LIGHTING PLOT

Property fittings required: Christmas tree lights
Several settings on open stage

ACT I Dawn

To open: General dawn lighting, concentrating on the Book

Cue 1	At end of Song 1 *Christmas tree lights up*	(Page 2)
Cue 2	**Mother Goose** tells story *Concentrate lighting to "family group"*	(Page 9)
Cue 3	**Gertie** enters *Lighting change to indicate start of "story" action*	(Page 9)
Cue 4	At opening of Scene 2 *Dark, sinister lighting*	(Page 15)
Cue 5	**Bigger Badder Wolf:** "... that scraggy bird" *Fade to spot on Miss Muffet, revert to previous lighting at end of verse*	(Page 20)
Cue 6	**Spider** eats curds and whey *Fade to Black-out, then return to opening "Book" scene lighting*	(Page 22)
Cue 7	**Wolves** grab **Bo Peep** *Fade to spot on Bo Peep, return to previous lighting at end of verse*	(Page 33)
Cue 8	**Fairy Lethargia:** "Magic the lot of them back" *Flash or snap Black-out, return to previous lighting*	(Page 34)
Cue 9	General exit after **Gertie** *Fade to Black-out, then up to Forest Lighting*	(Page 35)
Cue 10	**Fairy Lethargia** returns to decorations box *Fade to spot on star of fairy wand*	(Page 38)

ACT II

To open: Dim lighting on backcloth

Cue 11	As Scene 1 closes *Fade to Black-out, then up to cold lighting, with watery reflections, for Giant's Castle entrance*	(Page 40)
Cue 12	**Fairy Lethargia:** "Magic him into Tom Thumb" *Flash or snap Black-out, return to previous lighting*	(Page 44)
Cue 13	**Polly Flinders** lowers kettle *Fade to spot on Polly, revert to previous lighting at end of verse, fade to Black-out for scene change*	(Page 44)
Cue 14	Mime sequence *Effect of shifting, magical underwater light*	(Page 45)

Cue 15   **Tom Thumb** sees **Monster**   (Page 46)
          Fade to spot on Tom Thumb, revert to previous lighting at end
          of verse

Cue 16   At end of underwater sequence   (Page 46)
          Fade to Black-out, then return to Cue 11 lighting

Cue 17   **Fairy Lethargia:** "... is Two Number Spell"   (Page 47)
          Flash or snap Black-out, then revert to previous lighting

Cue 18   **Mother Goose** exits   (Page 51)
          Fade to Black-out, then up to Giant's Workshop scene lighting

Cue 19   **Bigger Badder Wolf** opens oven door   (Page 55)
          Red glow effect

Cue 20   **Giant** aims blow at **Jack Horner**   (Page 57)
          Fade to spot on Little Jack Horner, revert to previous lighting
          at end of verse

Cue 21   **Fairy Lethargia:** "Make us all able to fly"   (Page 58)
          Flash, Black-out, then full up for flying sequence—see text for
          suggested alternative methods

Cue 22   **Singers:** "This is her time to be brave"   (Page 59)
          Fade to Black-out, then up to Book scene lighting, with effect of
          dusk

Cue 23   **Fairy Lethargia** waves wand   (Page 62)
          "Magical" lighting changes, finishing up with bright, warm
          effect

Cue 24   **All:** "... find her sheep"   (Page 64)
          Flash

EFFECTS PLOT

ACT I

ACT II

Printed in Great Britain by Butler & Tanner Ltd, Frome and London